LOOKING and SEEING

Nalanda Miksang Contemplative Photography

WAY OF SEEING: VOLUME ONE

By

JOHN MCQUADE

and

MIRIAM HALL

ISBN: 0692383522
ISBN 13: 978-0692383520
Library of Congress Control Number: 2015903743
Drala Publishing
Madison WI
www.miksang.org
www.miksangwayofseeing.com
www.dralapublications.com

All images in this work are the creations of either John McQuade or Miriam Hall, with the exception of author photo of Miriam Hall, which is by Gloria Merriam.

This book is dedicated to our teachers Chögyam Trungpa Rinpoche
Sakyong Mipham Rinpoche
Vajra Regent Ozel Tenzin

May basic goodness dawn.
May the confidence of goodness be eternal.
May goodness be all-victorious.
May that goodness bring profound, brilliant glory.

ACKNOWLEDGMENTS

Writing a book of this scope and depth isn't easy. We went through many drafts and sought support from numerous readers, other students and teachers, and community.

First and foremost, we thank our teachers: Chögyam Trungpa Rinpoche, Sakyong Mipham Rinpoche and Varja Regent Ozel Tenzin. Without them, this would not exist.

On a more relative level, we want to thank our spouses, Alice and Ilana.

We want to give a huge, resonant thank-you to donors who made the funding of this book a no-debt proposition:

Tom Anderson and Mary Beth McBride, Augustine Baron, Lennie Birkett, Tamara Blenkhorn, Malini Dominey, Angel Eason, Araceli Esparza, Mark Edzards, Julie Einstein, Kathy Faas, Manon Francoeur, Ann and Darryl Hall, Ingrid Kelley, Jude Marion, Jerry McFarland, Jo Schaden, Mary Spike, Trudy Stern, Mark Sweet, and Jessica Winslow. To all of our Nalanda Miksang Society teachers and students: thank you for your enthusiasm, stories, and relentlessly loving encouragement to get this thing published.

Carolyn Gimian helped smoothed some doorways for us, and Andy Karr offered his support. Oliver Glosband eased us through the permissions process.

Maxine Sidran, in all her years of commitment with John to the Miksang way, gave invaluable feedback in the editing process. Our main editor, Lissa McLaughlin, jumped in with enthusiasm and clarity. Our production crew—Sara Ann Zola, Ilana Bryne, and many other people we don't even know the name of—made the final stages as painless as possible.

TABLE OF CONTENTS

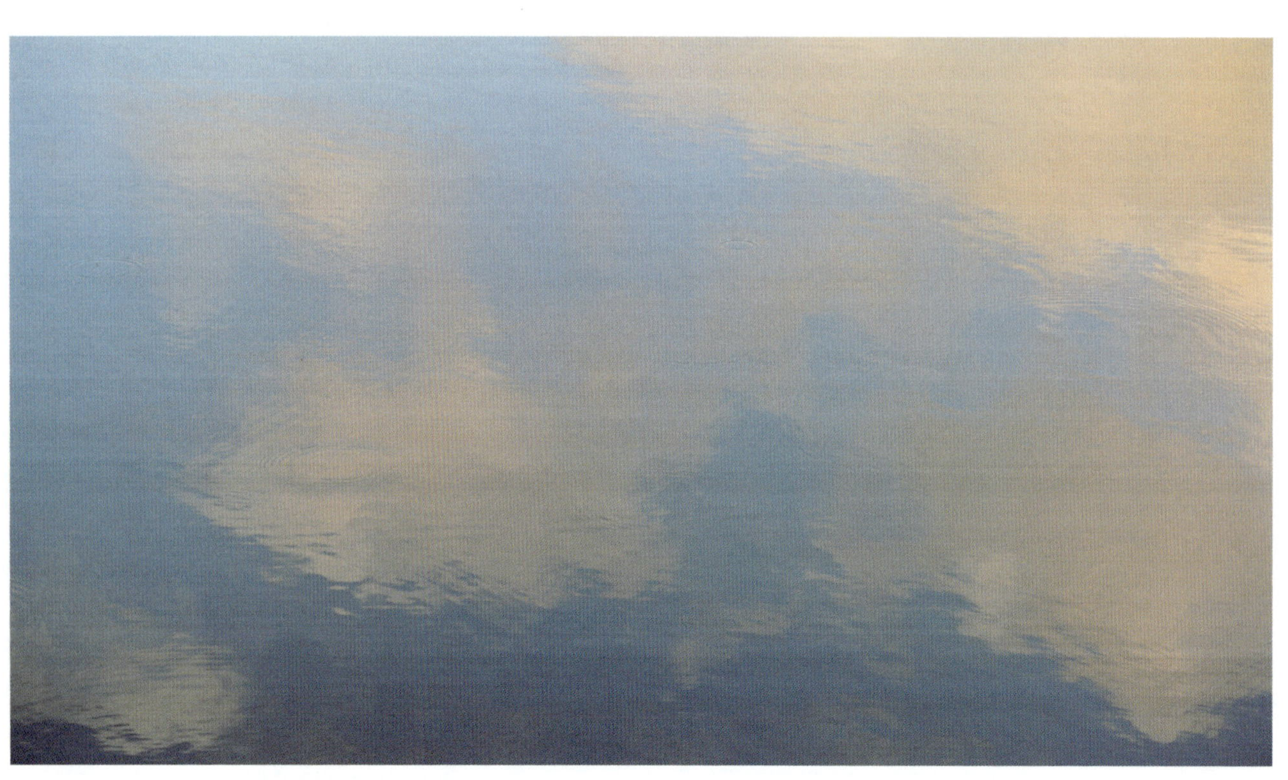

PREFACE

We think that we're 180 degrees from enlightenment, but we're only a few degrees off.
—from *Ruling Your World* by Sakyong Mipham

Once one of the oldest and most venerable camera clubs in North America invited me to present Nalanda Miksang as part of an ongoing series. To get a sense of that camera club's format, I attended one lecture. The presenter I watched recognized an institutionalized problem: a tendency towards photographic formula and technical skills in order to produce impressive images. His presentation was on how to break the rules of these photographic formulas to introduce more spontaneous creativity.

It was a good presentation, but I felt it missed the root issue. In my presentation, soon thereafter, I suggested that the most direct way to spontaneous creativity was not in "breaking the rules." It was in making contact with the world before there are rules at all.

In Nalanda Miksang, we work with what we see. This comes before rules.

And what do we see? One answer is that we see everything there is to see. There is a certain accuracy and insight in that statement. But in practical terms, it does not give us a way to work with the visual world, because everything we see is inexhaustible.

Nalanda Miksang invites us look around via the visual elements of the phenomenal world. For instance, is there color? Does seeing involve light? Do our eyes stop at a surface? Does the visual world involve space? And do we see something? These are some of the forms, or elements, of the visual phenomenal world.

Our path is a structured training to aid our liberation from a conventional, restricted, and glossed experience of the visual world, from the conventional, objective world of static things. Through training in the forms, we begin to enjoy a fresh experience of the visual world as a radiant, phenomenal display.

In practicing, we realize that the visual world is fresh and free, and that our experience can also be fresh and free. And more deeply, we realize that this freshness and freedom can point to something deep and profound—the spontaneous reality of the fresh and free. This connection with direct and clear perception becomes the basis for strong, vivid images, images that are artistic in the best sense: beautiful and transforming. And more, this practice is a basis for our lives.

Of course, this is not as easy as it sounds. To get here, we need to shift our orientation. For instance, photographers and all humans alike have many preconceptions concerning what we like and don't like; what we think is exciting and uninteresting; what we think is beautiful and not beautiful; what is or is not a good subject; what is or is not worth photographing; what technical formats and processes will create a great image; what will win a prize at a photographic contest; what will sell, etc. The endless trap of worries and projections goes on and on—and stops us from seeing the world awaiting us.

The challenge of Nalanda Miksang is to liberate ourselves by liberating the eye.

Here we are really talking about Enlightenment. Many spiritual traditions focus on this goal of Enlightenment. Some think it requires radical change, a complete switch from one reality to another. Yet Shambhala teacher Sakyong Mipham Rinpoche talks about our enlightenment being off by only a few degrees; we just have to shift our orientation a little, and the long-term consequences may be huge. Imagine a ship that shifts its trajectory 10 percent. At first, this change may seem tiny. But once across the ocean, it will arrive at a completely different destination than it would have had it maintained its original course.

One of the main understandings of Nalanda Miksang is this "few-degrees solution." Like changing our speed or momentum, this shift in orientation brings us to the radiant phenomenal world, and to the inherent radiance and goodness of our own lives.

This shift is one of the main teachings of Nalanda Miksang: shift your orientation from living in thing world, and wake to the visual world – the experienced world.

The "thing world" is the world we presume to be objective, the world that is just there. We work with the thing world in practical ways. For instance, we pick up a cup of coffee to drink it, but even this functional action puts us in touch with the world of experience. We experience the look of that cup, the glaze or pattern of the surface, the play of light, the feel of weight and smoothness; we experience that cappuccino's taste—sweet, bitter, hot but not too hot, etc. The experience world is the radiant, phenomenal world.

Nalanda Miksang wakes us to this world.

Every day when you wake up, your eyes open to the visual world. Nalanda Miksang is one way to work, and to play, with waking up, with seeing clearly, with making and sharing beautiful images, and with entering the Way of Seeing.

In our culture, we tend to default to thing world. It's like we're on autopilot. We hurtle down the freeway while we daydream about our upcoming vacation in Hawaii or thinking, *When she said that, I should have said this.* We hurtle through our lives to our certain deaths, so why not take some time to take some time? Just a shift of a few degrees to experience life as life, this beautiful life? It is for you and for everyone.

Miriam Hall is a senior teacher of Nalanda Miksang. Someone who wakes up to this world and knows the importance of making it available to everyone. Miriam showed up at one of my early workshops in Chicago—and then she just kept showing up. Wherever I taught, there she was. She attended the first official teacher training and became a Nalanda Miksang teacher. She kept showing up to further teacher trainings. At some point, I realized she was really there—she was there with the "there": she held the Nalanda Miksang teachings.

More and more, we worked together and were together in Nalanda Miksang. It was a natural situation. Eventually, I certified her as the first Nalanda Miksang Independent Teacher. What this means is that she can present the full range of the Nalanda Miksang teachings and can certify other teachers. But more importantly, though this certification may not be a mind-to-mind transmission in the Buddha dharma sense, it is a genuine, contemplative, beating heart–to–beating heart transmission.

We are both transmission students of Sakyong Trungpa Rinpoche and Sakyong Mipham Rinpoche. Though each of us has a deep commitment to the Shambhala Dharma tradition, neither of us believes that the contemplative way depends on any particular meditative school. Drawing on the wisdom of these traditions is simply another path to the Way, just as your path is your path, your everyday, ordinary life.

-John McQuade

To say that John and I differ in style and manner is a massive understatement. At some point on our path together, at a teacher training, John referred to me as the den mother of Nalanda Miksang and to himself as the stern father. I'm the artist and John's the philosopher. I am gregarious where he is shy. Hopefully, the balance between the two of us manifests as wisdom in these texts.

Teachings like these do not come around every day. Many teachings are available now that are based on or directly derived from dharma teachings. Plenty of people feel inspired to create teachings out of what has inspired them. What is different about Nalanda Miksang is its deep dedication to a specific way. Some people see this as a limitation—why have levels? Why say something is Miksang and something else isn't? Some find liberation in a way that uses structure to help us access our natural freedom.

One of the things John always reminds us is that the ultimate meditation instruction is: *Just be.* Good luck with that! For some reason, most of us seem to need assignments, instruction, guidelines, and even rules in order to nudge ourselves into recognizing what is "awake" and what isn't. Time and time again, online, in person, and in other ways, people have asked me the same question: Why this? Why not something else? Why can't we just see freely, without training or practice? The practical answer is: We do. All the time. But we don't see that we see.

Here is my more amorphous but personal answer: Here you are, looking at this book. Somehow, you feel drawn to it. Maybe a friend recommended it. Perhaps you liked the cover image. Maybe you have been inclined in this direction for a while. For whatever reason, now you are reading these words. That is a reason to give it a try. Not because we/Nalanda Miksang/Miksang is right. Not because it's the only way, because it isn't. It is this Way of Seeing. There are many paths to clear seeing, much less clear being! Insofar as Chögyam Trungpa and Shambhala are concerned, Miksang is the Way of Seeing that Chögyam Trungpa and the Vajra Regent oversaw and approved.

We often need to choose one way, though, at least for a while. One of our lineage teachers in Shambhala, Pema Chödrön, likes to say that in order to see if something is going to work for us, we need to practice it ten years. Ten years! I've been practicing Miksang now for over ten years. I am just starting to understand what my intuition landed upon a decade ago: for me, this is it. Maybe it's it for you too? It doesn't have to be the only way. Maybe it's just one of the many ways you will explore in your rich life on this planet.

What does it mean to choose a path, to commit to a teacher in the way that John and I have to Sakyong Mipham Rinpoche? Clarity. When a transmission comes down the line the way that Nalanda Miksang does, you can be assured that the product is clear. The methods are tested and strong. This does not mean it's the only way; however, it's a clear way—not all ways are.

I have the profound luck, karma, or auspiciousness (depending on how you cast it) to teach contemplative arts full-time. This great honor is at times an unwieldy necklace but always a buoyant blessing. Long ago, John made it clear to me that we do not have authority over Nalanda Miksang when we are given instruction or authorization to teach. It is not actually a gift given to us. Instead, we become a gift to Nalanda Miksang itself. Whenever I worry—about editing this book, meeting deadlines, answering the endless e-mails that are just one aspect of life as a Nalanda Miksang teacher—I return to this knowing. These teachings are endless gifts that remind me that I too can give endlessly.

Writing this book with John has been a difficult process—even for me, a self-identified writer! But it has also been a continuous gift. It is not easy to try to pin down what John has passed on and to articulate for myself what causes those great aha moments in students' eyes. It is, however, rewarding. We did fund-raising to get this book published. The contagious excitement of the society of teachers and practitioners helped buoy us in those moments when we considered just starting all over again.

This life is short. There is no starting the entirety of this lifetime all over again. And yet, following these teachings, through the direct experience of contemplative art, we can begin to really understand something. At a level neuroscience has measured, on the level of perception, every single millisecond we are starting again in some way. Now. Now and now, and again, now. Each "now" is access to richness, to a cornucopia of possibility that we cut off when we check out of the now.

I invite you to explore this volume. See what resonates for you. Question what doesn't and take your camera, or just your eyes, out for a walk and see if you can find some resonance there. Though this book is full of words, Nalanda Miksang is an experiential practice. It is not a bunch of concepts; it is a collection of methods to help us really see things as they are. How are those things, however they are at any given moment? Now. Now and now. And again, now.

-Miriam Hall

SECTION ONE:

OVERVIEW of the WAY

INTRODUCTION

This book is the first in a series of three. This book—and the two that will follow it—is a manual for the view and practice of Nalanda Miksang contemplative photography. From one point of view, because of the nature of transmission we will discuss in a moment, there is no substitute for an in-person workshop. We have established Nalanda Miksang teachers throughout North America, Europe, Australia, and online, so this more personal teaching is somewhat available.

At the same time, the many Nalanda Miksang weekend workshops and online weekly courses never cover the scope and depth of what is presented in this text. Through this manual, you can enter the Nalanda Miksang training, path, and realization. The realization of this path will be your brilliant images and enhancement of your brilliant life. It will work for you if you work through it.

Miksang is a Tibetan word that means *good eye*. Miksang was developed within the context of Chögyam Trungpa's dharma art and Shambhala teachings. Nalanda Miksang is the embodiment and expression of these teachings. Specifically, Nalanda Miksang is organized around Chögyam Trungpa's teachings on perception in both dharma art and Shambhala. His teachings on perception are a small but core part of his many teachings in dharma art. In turn, his dharma art teachings are a small part of his vast and profound dharma and Shambhala teachings.

Therefore, Nalanda Miksang presents a certain embodiment and expression of Chögyam Trungpa's multidimensional teachings. His dharma teachings are like Russian nesting dolls or, to use a dharma metaphor, they are like koans that open more koans. They are teachings that open more teachings. John's first dharma teacher sometimes said to him, "John, it is not enough to get the point. You need to get the point behind the point." The Nalanda Miksang teachings lean on a small facet of the perception and dharma art teachings of Chögyam Trungpa in order to access a vast and deep empowerment experience of the phenomenal world.

Daily life is the source of your empowerment, day in and day out.

This is the practical power of the contemplative arts.

TRANSMISSION

Generally, transmission refers to the direct and unbroken communication of a dharma realization. *Dharma* is a word that, in general, refers to things as they are. Dharma practices are there for us to experience insight (into things as they are), liberation (which arises from insight), and joy (the expression of liberation). An understanding of things as they are is said to pass from mind to mind, from warm hand to warm hand. Often transmissions are made from realized teachers to realized students. Such transmissions are within a lineage: those who receive it then hold the transmission. Sometimes it is a familial transmission, from one generation to the next.

More deeply, despite who is making the transmission or who is receiving it, the real transmission is from realization to realization. As the great Zen master Dōgen intuited: only a Buddha can know a Buddha. So there are also transmissions called *terma*: transmissions that flow directly from Buddha Mind, or lineage stream, to a realized teacher. We mention these variations on transmission because they all relate to both the activity of studying Nalanda Miksang and also to the sources of Nalanda Miksang.

BUDDHA DHARMA AND SHAMBHALA

John's unaccountable good fortune is to be a student of the great dharma master Chögyam Trungpa Rinpoche. Chogyam Trungpa focused on three pedagogical areas in his presentation of dharma teachings: the Buddha dharma, Shambhala, and Nalanda arts and education.

The Buddha dharma presents traditional Tibetan Buddhist teachings. The practice of the Buddha dharma is a practice of purification. The Buddha dharma view holds that our birthright reality is intrinsically pure. We are Buddha Nature—we are intrinsically awake and free—but more often than not, we do not realize this. Obstacles obscure this realization. The Buddha dharma path, to a degree, helps us overcome these blockages and barriers. Meanwhile, it also invites and draws upon the transforming power of original purity: Buddha Nature.

A master teacher of the Buddha dharma, Chögyam Trungpa is best known for the Shambhala dharma, which is a wisdom teaching that recognizes the intrinsic capacity of humans to manifest as a Good Society. Things as they are, are basically good. These teachings represent a lineage that goes back for millennia. Nalanda Miksang is a basic goodness practice, a recent and up-to-date embodiment of a timeless wisdom, because clear seeing guides us back to our own basic goodness. This is everyone's birthright: it manifests in all lives, households, and cultures.

Nalanda was one of the great Ancient Indian Buddhist universities. *Nalanda* was also Chögyam Trungpa Rinpoche's name for the overall organization of contemplative arts and education. Nalanda Arts say that as sentient humans, we are directly alive through our senses. Our senses connect us to the visual world, the audio world, and so on. We are sentient—we sense. And we can trust that sensing, that feeling, in a deep way. It is simple and also profound: our senses show us things as they are; our senses are not separate from things as they are. In fact, our senses can introduce us to relative manifestations of purity. As the Zen saying goes, one does not need to drink the ocean dry to know it is salty—or as Chögyam Trungpa says, "When we draw down the power and depth of vastness into a single perception, then we are discovering and invoking magic."

For Nalanda Miksang specifically, we relate to all of these Shambhala teachings as wisdom teachings. Your personal wisdom is not separate from the wisdom of the universe. This too is what we mean by basic goodness. The contemplative art of the eye that manifests this basic goodness is Miksang.

Shambhala also specializes in teachings on ordinary magic. These teachings join the secular and the sacred, the ordinary and the extraordinary. Because of these ordinary magic teachings, we realize that we do not need to go elsewhere—whether physically, in terms of changed circumstances, or spiritually, to find brilliance or be brilliant. The ordinary is not limited. It is magical. Your life is not just ordinary: it is ordinary magic.

CONTEMPLATIVE ARTS

Nalanda arts and education is a further expression of this view. We feel what it is to be alive. We can trust perception and feeling. It is that simple and also that profound. Our senses and the sensibility of the world are not-one and not-two; they effortlessly and incessantly commune with the way of things as they are. Not-one and not-two are ways of trying to break the dualism of one or the other. Dharma art is a gathering of art form and art-related practices that brings creative process into alignment with daily life and things as they are.

That is view, the overall understanding. When John first practiced in Chögyam Trungpa Rinpoche's Toronto Vajradhatu Center—now called Shambhala—the membership requirement was to practice sitting meditation for a minimum of thirty hours per month. These thirty hours had to include three *nyinthun*, defined as a daylong meditation session but was required to be three hours at Vajradhatu. Many people logged in the three nyinthun required by sitting three consecutive sessions on a single Sunday. In other words, nine hours with a few breaks.

To this day, John vividly recalls an experience after one such a daylong session. He was walking home to his apartment in the still-illuminated summer evening. In a subtle but definite way, the world seemed transformed. It was bright and vivid. The reds were more red, the blues were more blue and the whites were more white.

The juncture of the Buddha dharma path and the contemplative path is here, in that direct purity and joy of the senses. This overlap has manifested for millennia. Across centuries, Buddha dharma practitioners have experienced the delight and purity of their sensations and perceptions. They have also wondered if there is a way to embody and express this directly and personally, in more expressive ways than meditation and dharma talks.

Contemplative arts provide this way to this day.

THE CONTEMPLATIVE WAY

While meditators were meditating over the centuries, artists, craftspeople, and ordinary folk began to sense the subtle but deep implications of their activities. In a regular, human way, they synchronized their bodies and minds with their activities. Through their craft and art, they expressed simplicity and directness. Some of them became interested in the practice of meditation, which illuminated their artistic activity. Many did not, remaining outside Buddha dharma or formal contemplative communities.

Contemplative and meditative practices work well together. Yet both the meditative and the contemplative have their own integrity and can be done alone.

You may or may not be interested in the ways of the meditative traditions: hours of sitting meditation, mantras, koans, postures, chanting, visualization, and so forth. You might or might not be intrigued by the profound views on the nature of reality, like impermanence, emptiness, the Dao, and so forth. However we express it, we all want to be fully alive in this life.

This is the contemplative view, orientation, and practice. Contemplative photography is a simple and direct way to engage this simple and direct way. See the brilliant world, and make and share brilliant mages. You can find your way, simply by living and sensing, to the direct connection. The *direct connection* is the transmission of your brilliance to your brilliance.

The contemplative view can run much deeper than even these points. But the simplicity of this—and other contemplative arts practices—is that it helps us connect. We receive and give. In other words, we open the door to transmission. We are in touch, and we are touched. We are connected and in communion. This is not abstract. It is direct, sensual, and now. It can be a practice and a way of life.

Still the question remains: How is this practice and realization transmitted? For now, let's keep it simple and present two ways: articulating the view and practicing the pedagogy.

The view has already been presented, and how we embody it is through practice.

For instance, in this text, you will be given assignments with specific topics. I have noticed during the reviews that are crucial to training that people sometimes present images that are Nalanda Miksang images yet don't represent the specific assignment when doing the first few assignments. Often, they are good examples of assignments that have not yet been presented. How is this possible?

It is possible because pure perception does not know about or care about Nalanda Miksang training. Pure perceptions emerge as perceptions of themselves.

Nalanda Miksang is a skillful, contemplative, artistic way of channeling our intrinsic depth and power of pure perception. Through it, we experience personal joy and artistic brilliance that can be embodied and shared as an image.

THE WAY OF SEEING

The idea of the *Way*, or *Path*, is common to many Eastern spiritual traditions. As path and practice, a way encourages us to see the fundamental goodness, enlightenment, and joy in our everyday activities. Meditative and contemplative traditions provide connection with the Way through their specific ways. There are many contemplative art ways. There is the way of *Cha* (tea ceremony), the way of calligraphy, the way of *Kyudo* (archery), the way of haiku, and so forth.

We hope that by offering you Nalanda Miksang training, you can enter clear seeing, purify your perception, and make brilliant images. The basic view of Nalanda Miksang is a way of discovering and expressing magic. Along the way, you will encounter ordinary magic, connect with basic goodness, and affirm and enjoy the miracle of your life that is every person's birthright. We hope you will share that life with others as a way of working together for a good society.

Maybe your agenda sounds different than this. You may only be interested in making stronger photographs. Maybe you have different spiritual views. Whatever it is you are interested in is fine. These teachings are an offering and you may receive them in whichever way will be of benefit.

If you just want to make stronger images, following the way of Nalanda Miksang will help you generate thousands upon thousands of vivid, beautiful images, effortlessly. You can have your cake and eat it too. This is part of the magic of this Way.

Perhaps you are interested in post-processing work with Photoshop. These projects also benefit from a strong image. We just work from the inside out, with the knowledge that every image begins with perception. Nalanda Miksang focuses on strong first perceptions. You will naturally make a strong image if you start with a strong perception.

You might be interested in the contemplative aspect of Nalanda Miksang. Here, the images are also important. Clear seeing is vivid, and the images made from clear seeing are beautiful. They provide direct feedback on how well you are connecting with clear perception. Bringing beauty into the world produces goodness for others to experience. And where does that beauty come from? Connection with both the ordinary world and the phenomenal world.

The fact is, regardless of your personal agenda, the images are the easy part. Accumulating brilliant images is a piece of cake. The more challenging part is realizing your birthright heart's capacity to be a fulfilled, sentient human being. Still, even this realization is almost immediately available. Just like that, you can become in touch with and touched by things as they are. This is what it is to be a contemplative. Once in touch, you realize your unique and personal wisdom is the same wisdom of things as they are. Hopefully, this practice takes you deeply enough that you begin to understand it is always true—not just when photographing Nalanda Miksang, but in all of your life.

How?

PHOTOGRAPHY

Photography is a focal point of Nalanda Miksang practice. After all, this is an art of contemplative photography rather than the art of contemplative basket weaving, which was, by the way, an ancient Christian contemplative practice.

Nalanda Miksang teaches you to make an equivalent image of a true first perception. We say equivalent because no artistic form can exactly reproduce a perception. In part, this is what makes this practice contemplative.

In some other artistic and photographic practices, you make an equivalent of some preexisting idea. There is nothing inherently wrong with this; it is another method of doing photography and making images. But this is not our contemplative way. It does not come down to a contemplative way versus a technological way. It is not that crude or dualistic. Both practices involve the technology of photography, making images, and equivalence.

The difference is more a matter of intention and orientation, no matter how much or what technology you use. Why are you photographing? What keeps you going? Is it the thrill of making a great image? Is it the energy of the creative process in making a brilliant image? Is it recognition from others of your powerful images? Is it the process more than the product: just being in the visual world and making images along the way? Is it a feeling of being connected to something deeper? Is it the joy of this deep but ordinary connection?

This is all good. The thrill of making a great image is not less valid than the sense of something deeper. It is more a matter of balancing all these interests, and not fixating on a particular aspect of the whole process.

Your aspiration may be to make creative images or to be a good photographer. There is no problem with that in terms of contemplative photography. The contemplative view is simply that you cannot be more creative than creation. The way to spontaneous creativity, sustained equanimity, and subtle joy is not through a limited individual and conceptual project, but through the open ways of the Way, in this case, the Way of Seeing. All the great creative artists and photographers fit into this. At the heart of their artistic work—whatever one's professed viewpoints are—we can discern this spark of creation that is connected to reality.

The camera plays at least three roles in contemplative photography. It is our format, our medium, and our craft. In contemplative arts, we try to keep format, media, and craft very basic.

This is in contrast to the fine arts. Fine arts require many years of training in sophisticated forms. You cannot become a concert pianist without years of discipline and instruction. Think of an orchestra: they play a score from an artistic genius; they have a trained conductor, many specialized instruments, and trained musicians.

The forms of contemplative art are usually very ordinary: the brushes, ink, and paper of calligraphy; haiku's seventeen syllables; everyday implements in the tea ceremony, etc. Training and skill are also very basic. It is often the case that a novice produces a masterpiece. This is certainly the case in Nalanda Miksang. In a beginning weekend workshop, we can see practitioners produce masterpiece images.

In our lives, the camera is a simple, available, and everyday format. It is widely available in many forms. It is not difficult to master the basics. It is already a part of popular culture. These aspects of the camera make it ideal for contemplative practice. You do not need the discipline of mastering an artistic form. With the camera, you can directly use it to manifest a contemplative way with the world.

There are also specifics to photography that lend themselves to the contemplative way: working with direct visual contact, working with the now as now, the way of joining the perceiver and the perceived, the immediate impact of image equivalence, and so forth.

And then the images themselves are crucial to this contemplative practice. They are the means, the expression, the way of learning, the artistic crystallization and social media of the practice, and much more.

Contemplative photography is one of the first purely modern forms of contemplative art. There are many current artistic disciplines that have a contemplative influence: dance, poetry, and so forth. But there is a difference between influence and form. Nalanda Miksang is a modern contemplative photographic art form.

VIEW AND PRACTICE

The medium of Nalanda Miksang is photography. But the *way* is contemplative. This is what we mean by *contemplative photography*. Our approach is to start with visual perception. Our view is that a strong image is made from a true first perception. So our main focus is on those true first perceptions.

A *perception* is a personal experience and a connection with the visual world. A perception is the intimate relationship between the perceiver and the perceived. We see something—it is that simple.

It is obvious. We see something. But here's where it's profound: the contemplative practice is to transform the obvious, ordinary experience into an appreciation of the ordinary as extraordinary, the appreciation of it for what it is—the ordinary magic of being alive. It turns out that seeing itself is ordinary and yet completely miraculous. How can we tap into that understanding?

You just need to connect with and appreciate the ordinary miracle of visual perception. This brings simple joy in your life. It's as simple as that. But here's where simple is profound: all of our patterns work against that joy. We need the ways of the Way. That is the paradox: even though true perception is an ongoing given, most of us need to engage a way, a path, to overcome the momentum of pattern and connect with things as they are.

When we feel connected and wholesome, we feel alive. Connected can feel good and intimate and also on the edge, exhilarating—ordinary and extraordinary at the same time.

Nalanda Miksang photography, like many contemplative and Buddhist forms, offers an intensive, structured training. There are many assignments and teachings. The assignments are designed to give you the visual tools for creating vivid images and appreciating the visual feast of your life, to empower the visual world to wake you up from your half-blind patterns to the full kaleidoscope of your creative life.

The basic view of Nalanda Miksang can be found in Chögyam Trungpa's Shambhala teachings, from *Shambhala Sacred Path of the Warrior*:

> [Y]our own wisdom as a human being is not separate from the power of things as they are. They are both reflections of the unconditioned wisdom…Therefore there is no fundamental separation or duality between you and your world. When you experience these two things together, as one, so to speak, then you have access to tremendous vision and power in the world—you find that they are inherently connected to your own vision, your own being. That is discovering magic.

The specific view of Nalanda Miksang is that the practice is not to *construct* a clear perception and image but to *connect* with an already-existing, clear perception and make an equivalent image.

Our perceptions are not separate from the creative power of the perceived, a.k.a. the phenomenal world. This harmonization of the perceiver and the perceived (you and the world) feels good. It feels wholesome because it is an experience of the whole, when we are used to surviving on just part.

In Shambhala teachings, this ordinary miracle is said to be basic, but as in basic goodness. In Nalanda Miksang, pure perception is a specific manifestation of this basic goodness. But if it is so basic and so good, why don't we usually have access to it?

The drag of our patterns and the speed of conventional life obscure and block our appreciation of and our access to this naturally relaxed vision. We find ourselves caught in an overwhelming vortex of demand and distraction.

And sometimes, even when we do access natural vision, our reaction is numbness: we tune out or zone out or just get by the best we can. Sometimes, we default to stimulants or sedatives, whether drugs or entertainment, that simulate the vitality of life. Then we are out of touch, if not actually sleepwalking through life.

Most of us live the best we can within the demands, circumstances, and aspirations of our life. This is heroic and is to be deeply honored. Yet we may long for some relief, some sense of peace, joy, and fulfillment beyond the day in, and day out demands.

Nalanda Miksang is a practice that cuts through these constraining patterns. What it puts into play is the ordinary miracle of pure perception. At minimum, it is a time out to tune in to the timeless time our fresh, ordinary ongoing life.

The practical view of Nalanda Miksang is that we do not have to become creative. We just need to relax and work with the natural creativity of things as they are. We don't create the world, but we can tune in to its power of creativity when we realize we are already artists. This is the way of contemplative art.

Just like in contemplative art versus fine art, in this contemplative practice, you do not need to enter a specialized meditative or spiritual practice. There are many spiritual teachings and practices that guide the transition from stress to ease, from confusion to wisdom. We honor and recommend the genuine versions of these transmissions, teachings, and practices. They are direct ways to liberation. And the Nalanda Miksang practice resonates with many of these genuine meditation ways. But our practice is its own way, a contemplative way—the Way of Seeing.

The main practice of Nalanda Miksang is the harmonization of the perceiver (you) and the perceived (the phenomenal world) through clear seeing/pure perception. This harmonization is the contemplative way of peace and joy. This is the main point of Nalanda Miksang: peace, joy, liberation.

The specific practice of Nalanda Miksang is the skillful means of generating beautiful equivalent images of these radiant pure perceptions.

Our approach is to connect with a strong first perception. This focus on a strong first perception joins the main practice—harmonization of perceiver and perceived—with the specific practice of generating beautiful images.

After all this, again we return to simplicity. As Shambhala teacher Pema Chödrön reminds us, we must start where we are. We cannot begin with fantasy, or even hope for artistic brilliance. We must begin with honest, lived experience, and work through our struggles to find the clarity of the perception underneath. Balancing practice and view, we come to the depth of Nalanda Miksang.

Dharma teachings always bring together view and practice. The traditional analogy is that these are the two wings of a bird. You need both wings. Sometimes we desperately feel that we just want to be fulfilled. We just want the strong and vivid images. However, that is like taking a journey with no direction.

A structured practice like Nalanda Miksang gives us commitment and a sense of adventure. Let yourself open to the Way. You need a direction home, and view is that map. View and practice—with these wings, you soar through the Way.

CONCLUSION

You can access Nalanda Miksang contemplative photography in whatever way works for you. The visual world does not concern itself with your personal intentions. Red is red. Blue is blue. White is white. This is a direct way of liberation. In this direct way, you can be free of you and be free to be you. You can just free flow with the phenomenal world and make brilliant images.

This is the skillful means of the contemplative art ways: your ordinary life perceptions and experiences can open you to the same profound connections that the great dharma and Shambhala teachings present. This is the contemplative transmission: you practice in order to find your brilliance, which was there all along. Your life as your life is liberation.

Nalanda Miksang is a way to make many brilliant images. And that is good. It feels good because it connects you with basic goodness: things as they are, from which you are not separate. Nalanda Miksang becomes Nalanda Miksang when you become you. The images are a way to your way as the Way: the Way of Seeing.

POSSIBLE WAYS TO USE THIS BOOK

Nalanda Miksang is:

1. Only one way of practicing contemplative photography;
2. More a practice than a product, and
3. Best experienced as a person-to-person transmission, like most dharma teachings.

While a book, a website, or an online course will never replace an in-person program, we hope that this offering will help pique—and hopefully satisfy—some of your interest in Nalanda Miksang.

And here are three ways of proceeding with this material:

1. **Read the book straight through.** This is the way it is intended. Assignments in this book appear in the order they are presented in classes, interspersed with contemplation and reflection sections. Since the teachings are experience based, we strongly suggest that you practice as you go.

2. **Do just the assignment sections.** Read through sections one and two, then move into the third section, Color as Color. The first two sections contain important teachings involving one of the wings of Nalanda Miksang. You might then move along to the fifth section, which presents Light, Texture, and Pattern, and then end with seventh section, Space and Dot in Space. You can always come back later and read the contemplations—or not at all if you simply aren't interested. This is your path if you are mainly interested in making strong photographs and exploring the visual world experientially.

3. **Read the contemplative sections only.** We recommend this way the least. The teachings really are based in practice, but this might be your path if you are primarily here for the dharma teachings and less interested—at least at this point—in photography.

Regardless, we suggest you read through the whole of Section Two: Entering the Way. If you skip right to the first assignment, Color as Color, in Section Three (which we know you are already excited for), you miss out on important guidelines, suggestions and teachings. Your patience with the view helps support and deepens your practice.

And in terms of sharing your practice with others? Create a local group to work through the book together. Invite authorized teachers to present an in-person workshop. Visit us online through social media platforms and websites, listed in the appendix. Many more images, showing the full range of these assignments, are available through our website and the book's website. Please visit and socialize, building Enlightened Society together through practice.

www.miksang.org
www.miksangwayofseeing.com

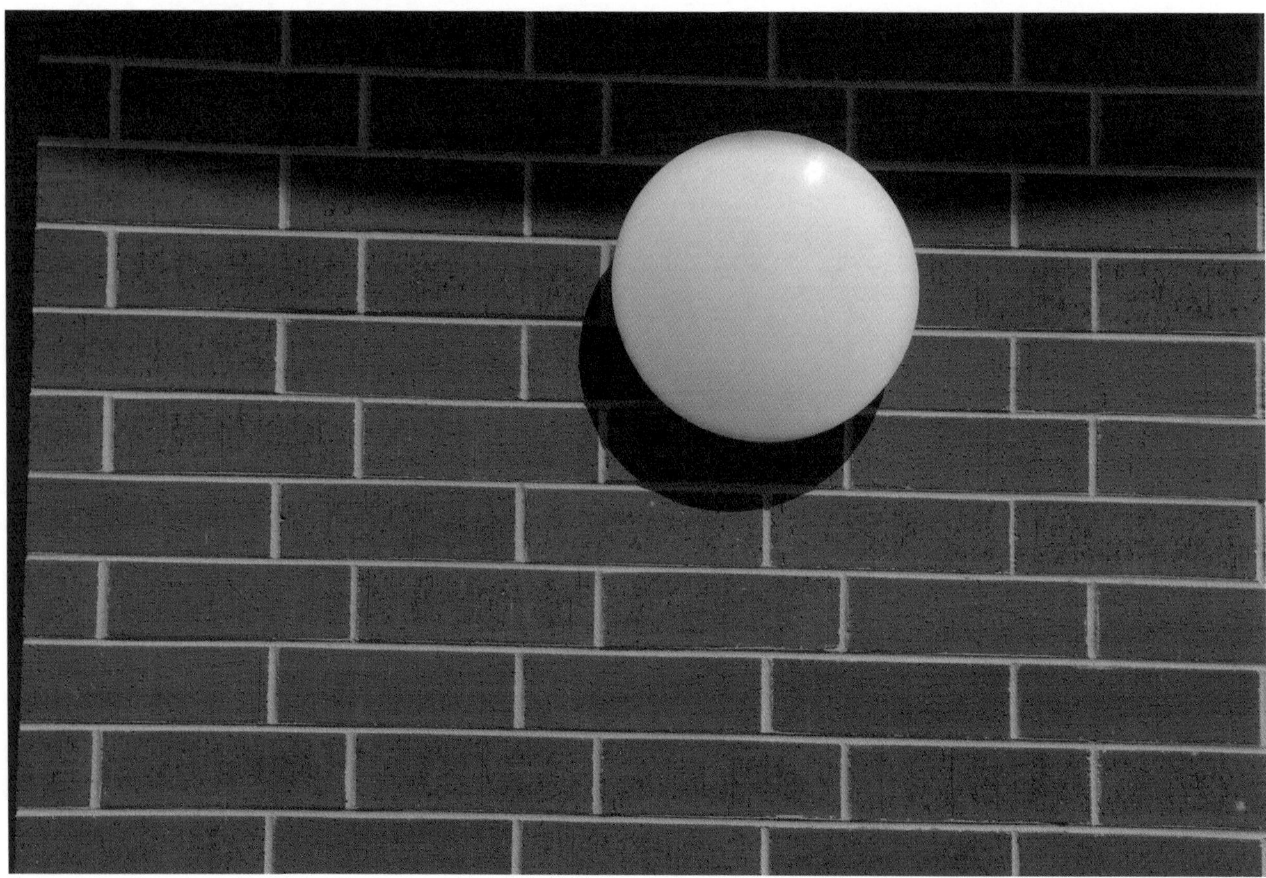

PERSONAL STORY: JOHN

When I began meditation and Miksang contemplative photography practice, I lived a routine, A, B, C life. I was a graduate student, and my apartment was a long walk from the subway station. My day always began at point A—the apartment—then, the long walk to point B—the subway station—and then a train ride to point C—the university. At the time, it seemed to me that only when I arrived at point C did life begin. The path from point A to B and from point B to C was only a functional necessity. And it was the same in reverse.

It was while I was in transit that I first noticed the effects of my meditation and contemplative photography practices. During the A-to-B walk in particular, I began to notice things. Nothing major—just ordinary occurrences changing ever so subtly over time because of circumstances, weather, lighting, etc. They had been there the whole time; it was just that I had finally started to notice them.

Sometimes I noticed laundry or birds on a clothesline. Although at first glance, all the houses and yards seemed similar, everyone's front yard was a little different. And the front yards changed over time. More and more, I realized what I was seeing was not the same old, same old. In fact, it was always fresh and interesting. These walks became a highlight of my day, not only because they were refreshing but also because they taught me something subtle yet decisive. I came to understand that I was seeing the way of the world: the way the world actually is.

SECTION TWO:

ENTERING the WAY

Either you look and see beyond language - as a first perception - or you see the world through the filter of your thoughts, by talking to yourself. Everyone knows what it is like to feel things directly. Intense emotions...don't have a language. They are too intense in the first flash...Synchronizing mind and body is looking and seeing directly beyond language...you can see on the spot with wakefulness. Your eyes begin to open wider and wider, and you see that the world is colorful and fresh and so precise, every sharp angle is fantastic.

- Chögyam Trungpa Rinpoche, Shambhala Sacred Path of the Warrior

THE MIND-SET OF PRACTICE

Here are some main points that we will explain in this section. The first three are right motivation, right view, and right intent. These three have to do with how we approach our practice and life in a big way. The second three—synchronization, the flash of perception, and forming an equivalent image—have to do specifically with Nalanda Miksang.

MOTIVATION, VIEW, AND INTENT

Motivation and view are the background of contemplative practice. You don't have to get too deep into motivation to simply begin. However, contemplative photography can be a way to connect with the ordinary magic of being fully human and completely awake.

Motivation

At the beginning, any motivation is fine, but it is helpful and insightful to consider your motivation. It indicates where you are, who you are, and where you are going. That can change from shoot to shoot, and over years of practice. The deepening of motivation is a lifelong practice. Continually touching base with your current motivation(s) is a powerful aspect of contemplative practice.

View

View is not theory. View is an orientation. It sees the possible journey and points you in the right direction. If you are not pointed in the right direction, as we have said, then it is unlikely that you will reach any destination.

View is connected to fulfillment; it is both the overview of the journey and the understanding of the journey. As you take the journey, you understand the journey. With understanding comes fulfillment and insight. This is called holding the view.

Nalanda Miksang speaks of a general view and an instructional view. One of our general views is that clear seeing is our birthright. Clear seeing is not something you achieve through Nalanda Miksang, but it is something this practice can help you realize and reconnect to. This deep and abiding resource is available to all of us.

An example of the instructional view would be the teachings on the Three Levels of Perception or the teachings of Looking and Seeing from Chögyam Trungpa.

At this point, it is helpful to know the general view of the Nalanda Miksang path and recognize the underpinning instructional views.

Intent

Intent is the most critical part of entering the Way of Seeing. Intent is not so much a marshaling of will as a turning of the mind. Intent can be considered a form of discipline, but in the contemplative practices, it is the discipline of relaxation.

SYNCHRONIZATION, THE FLASH OF PERCEPTION, AND LOOKING AND SEEING

Two practices connect us with clear perception: the synchronization of eye and mind, and the flash of perception. You begin a session with the intent of synchronization, or you can invoke it with an exercise. At some point in that session, you experience the flash of perception. A flash of perception can also appear on its own, without warning or preparation on your part. But the flash of perception exercise can help you become more familiar with it.

Synchronization requires you to be practical. In order to act out your intention, you need to schedule and prepare for your shoot and practice. The night before you go out to shoot, begin your practice by checking your camera. In the contemplative disciplines, instruments for practice are treated with respect, whether the brush of the calligrapher or the bow of the Kyudo archer. So check your camera: Is the battery charged? Is the lens clean? Is the memory card empty? Does it have enough room for more images?

SYNCHRONIZATION

A contemplative mind is the natural mind for appreciating our life. Intent is the practical first connection.

In Nalanda Miksang, synchronization is the state where eye, mind, and world are in the same place at the same time. They are in harmony. When they are harmonized, perception is clear. There is no struggle. Your eye and mind are not distracted. They are in the same place at the same time. You experience simplicity and directness.

When you start your shoot, you are not going for a stroll. You are practicing the art of seeing. Clear seeing and synchronization of eye and mind occur together. Synchronization is ongoing; it occurs throughout the session. It includes paying spacious but specific attention to the details of seeing, and paying attention to the specifics of craft.

The aim is to see just that and just so (e.g., just that color). That color fills the whole eye, the whole mind and is, for that moment, the whole visual world. You have the experience of what it is like to be whole, to be in harmony. This is the experience you are actually photographing: synchronizing and perceiving. The subject of your photograph is this experience. In other words, the subject is not color—it is color as color, your direct, pure experience of color. We arrive at this through synchronization.

At the beginning of your shoot, you rouse the intent of clear seeing and synchronization. In the first assignment, we intend to see color—color as color.

An unsynchronized mind finds it difficult to fully engage, to appreciate color or any other element of the visual. The same is true of any of the practicalities of our daily living. When you wash the dishes, are you doing it with simplicity, clarity, and appreciation? Or with a haphazard, distracted, and habitual mind and body? No matter what our task, we can find delight through clear perception and direct appreciation.

When you are ready, prepare your camera, making sure you have all your supplies, and go to your location with the intent to see clearly. But don't use your camera yet. Allow yourself space and time to settle into attentive relaxation. With the intent to see color, start walking and looking, walking and looking. With the intent to see color, allow your eye, mind, and body to synchronize.

You may not feel very synchronized and settled. You may feel awkward, hesitant, and distracted, or full of excitement and anticipation. Your attention may be carried away by all kinds of thoughts and emotions, including thoughts about the session itself, how it is going or not going. You worry about doing the assignment right. All kinds of attractions may distract your eye; you may see everything except color!

Remember: intent is not an act of will. It is a turning of the mind, an orientation. Trying to see clearly is not exactly intent. We tend to try too hard, and the harder we try, the less relaxed we are, which creates further obstacles. So have a light touch with intention. In the long run, this helps you develop confidence that clear seeing is a natural occurrence. Until then, start with the conscious practice of attentive relaxation.

SYNCHRONIZATION EXERCISE

Give some attention to other aspects of your experience, such as, the rhythm of your walking. For a while, settle in on this rhythm of your physical presence. Or attend to the sounds throughout the space: bird sounds, traffic sounds, voices, jets, etc. If it helps, stop and sit to experience this, or stand without moving. Use these fleeting sounds to relax into a vaster sense of space—a surrounding sense of the space you are walking through, in which everything is manifesting. Here you are relaxing and synchronizing mind and body. This can support synchronizing your eye and mind. It also takes your focus off your eyes.

Then, after synchronizing through other senses, begin to see color without raising your camera. Start with the practice of noticing, just noticing color here and there. The more you give intention to noticing, the less your attention will be distracted by other concerns. More and more, you are synchronized with color, and so you will see more color. The more you notice color, the more your noticing will intensify the process of synchronization. This is how it works. Your eye and mind become synchronized with seeing color.

The world is full of colors. From a true contemplative view, this noticing is not quite the *real* looking. It is looking at, when there is still a strong sense of separation between the one who is looking and that which is being looked at. But this is part of the contemplative process; it is part of the synchronization process, looking for color and looking at color.

When it feels right, if you want, you can start to use your camera. Work with color and camera. Soon, you see and meet the colors. Now you are synchronized and you move from noticing—looking at—to the process of looking and seeing, the prime features in the process of clear seeing.

LOOKING AND SEEING

Looking is the moment of contact with what you perceive. In this case, the contact is with color as color. Looking is connection. You only see what you look at, and this looking identifies the perception. It is contact with just *that*: just *that* perception, just *that* color.

In this contact, there is a moment of being *there* with *that*. *That* color *there*. The emphasis is not on *this* (oneself), but rather, *this* is fully present to *that* perception. For an immeasurable moment, there is a full experience of synchronization. Experience becomes relatively nondualistic. This indicates a contemplative experience.

You can hold to this perception even as you are held by it. In *looking*, the *eye* is stopped or held. It is held in a direct simplicity and attentiveness. And when the *eye* is stopped, the *mind* is stopped; it is held in direct simplicity and attentiveness. Wonder and/or appreciation arise. Mind thinks not just *That* but also *That's interesting*.

Now we move from looking to seeing, from contact to communication. We move from registering just that color, to just that/just so. *Just that* is an experience of it over there. *Just so* is an experience of personal connection: things as they are with us as we are. We begin to understand what that perception is saying. We don't just notice the perception; we commune with it. We appreciate it. This is on-the-spot contemplation. This is contemplative eye and mind in the Way of Seeing.

Seeing explores the qualities of the perception. (*This is not just red but a certain shade, vibrancy, hue of red.*) Seeing may note other visual elements, such as contrast with other colors or elements like light or space, coolness or hotness. To the mind, these may suggest feeling tones: it's soothing, or it's electrifying. This mind impact can produce thoughts such as *fire-engine red*. These features, and many more, comprise the layered dimensions that articulate seeing.

This perceptual feature of seeing—moving from just that to just that/just so and from *That* to *That's interesting*—fulfills the process of perception. It is also the ground or bridge for composing the visual image. The visual image then communicates the communion with the perception.

Now, through the practice of synchronization you have entered the Way of Seeing. You are looking and seeing and making contemplative images.

FLASH OF PERCEPTION

Synchronization is somewhat conditioned; it is gathered through practices of intent, noticing, looking, and seeing. For instance, for the first assignment, you contemplate color as color. But something else might happen in the midst of a session—color suddenly pops in the field of your experience. It catches your eye. We all have this experience. Some blur catches our eye, and as we turn, we register it as a bird. This can be more obvious with sounds: a bang shocks us, and we realize it was a car door slamming shut. Such flashes are a different kind of opening than the slower, softer openings of synchronization —more sudden, sharp, and clear.

This may happen with any of the assignments in this book. Rather than you noticing it, a something comes to you. We call this the *flash of perception*. Sometimes we refer to it as the *gap of perception*. This points to the feeling it can invoke, one of sudden and total groundlessness.

Flash of perception is decisive for the Nalanda Miksang Way of Seeing. It is somewhat less conditioned than synchronization. It catches your eye before you have a thought about it. It is free of your thoughts and the set of filters that supports your thoughts. It is a direct communication from the world, always fresh and free.

This fresh and free way perception fills life with adventure and appreciation. This is the Nalanda Miksang now moment.

It's simple and shocking, and also ordinary and extraordinary. It is different than noticing. It is the natural way perception manifests, but we don't usually connect with it. We don't usually appreciate it. Flashes of perception have the same final effect as synchronization, though a different felt quality. For a timeless moment, your whole perception is that color—just that color. This is the *complete* synchronization. This is the *pure* looking and seeing.

This gap is (relatively) uncontrived and unconditioned. In this sense, you do not produce it, nor do your efforts, or even your intent. Yet it happens within the field of your intent, perception, and experience. It is very personal and intimate.

Although you do not produce it, paradoxically, you can solicit it. This is a deeper aspect of right intent. In part, Nalanda Miksang trains you to become a lightning rod for the flash of perception.

Notice the qualities of this perception mind: lightweight, buoyant, and awake. At the same time, it is not purely abstract. On the contrary, it couldn't be more sensuous: color. Pure color. Here and now.

Connecting with the flash of perception, with this flash of color, you stay with it and then make an equivalent image, an image that embodies the form, content, and qualities of that flash. Staying with this perception, dwelling in its presence, and discerning its qualities are parts of the art of seeing. The crafting of an equivalent image is the next step in the Nalanda Miksang practice.

You make an image, let go, and move on. You continue to work with the intent of seeing: recognizing and working with these openings of perception, whether through synchronization or flash.

Notice that the flash of perception also works with you. There is an accumulation, momentum, and intensification. It is easier to tune in, to go with it. The flash of perception is real synchronization of eye and mind. As you connect with synchronization, the process is more stabilized, more effortless. The distractions and conventions of the discursive mind dissolve and are put out of play.

Now the session becomes delight and adventure. You embody and experience the positive and affirmative power of intent, clear seeing, and pure perception: a free-floating buoyancy and pliancy of mind, a natural clarity and free-flowing intensity, a sense of joy and well-being. The open eye goes through the world connecting effortlessly with the solicitations of color.

I live in a neighborhood on the near east side of Madison, Wisconsin. I can walk to most of my major needs: grocery cooperative, credit union, hardware store, many restaurants, etc. So I spend a lot of time walking in a very functional way.

Early on in my Miksang practice, I was struggling with finances. I was on my way to the credit union to try and extend a line of credit. I was completely immersed in my frustration, my fear and anguish. I almost bumped into a couple of beings along the way: a blind man and his cane, and a dog waiting for an owner outside a café. Even those didn't slow me down. The more absorbed I got, the faster I walked, my head down.

Then, all of a sudden, I looked up, not even sure why. The only way I can explain it is to say that I suddenly knew I had to look up. A single sunbeam was shining through a tree's branches, brightening a yellow maple leaf completely. I immediately stopped in my tracks—something was communicating with me. I was filled with a sense of joy and lightness, literally, as if that beam were heading through the leaf and into my eyes and heart. I had never experienced anything like it. I dropped all my worries for a single moment.

They returned of course—I still had a block to go to the credit union and an awkward appointment to sit through—but I was forever changed. I didn't need to take a photo. That moment pierced me, and the only reason I was even ready to receive it was because of my fledgling practice. I took no picture. I didn't need to.

FLASH OF PERCEPTION EXERCISE

We have a very simple exercise that can help you recognize the flash of perception more easily. This exercise simulates and stimulates a flash of perception. Try it before you set out on your first color session, and anytime you want to refresh your connection to the phenomenal world. It is incredibly simple but profound.

It is also one of our very few lessons in what others might call *composition*, which we refer to as how to craft an equivalent image of a flash of perception. This lesson applies to the Way of Seeing through both the practices of synchronization and flash of perception.

First, go with your camera to a large, secure, and contained space, perhaps a large room like a Buddhist shrine room or a gymnasium or, if outdoors, an alleyway or a spacious parking lot. If necessary, you can even do it in your living room.

Close your eyes and slowly spin around so you do not know your exact orientation. Pause. Now open your eyes and notice what flashes as a perception. What do you first see? It does not matter what you see. Just notice that you are seeing. You are not looking for color or any specific perception. Try to stay with the perception that catches your eye. It usually will be specific. Before labeling, before you can even say what it is, your eye is drawn to something initially. What was it drawn to?

PHOTOGRAPHING A FLASH OF PERCEPTION

One of our slogans is "Fill the frame with the flash of perception." Another way to say this is fill the frame with the clear perception. Contemplative photography teachers Andy Karr and Michael Wood have also called this "forming an equivalent image."

Fill the camera viewfinder or screen with the specific and unique elements of the perception delivered in that flash. The perception does not necessarily have to happen where you are standing. It happens wherever it is, so you may not make the image where you are standing. More often than not, if you shoot from where you are standing when you receive the flash, you will include many elements that were not part of the perception. Recall that the perception is quite definite. Stay with that.

This usually means you walk over to where the perception appeared, and then fill the viewfinder or screen with that perception. This is how you make an image of a flash of perception.

Perception does not happen in the three-dimensional space that you walk through. It happens in perceptual space. What does that mean? We will explore this more deeply later, but for now, suffice to say that your eyes cut through space and draw a specific perception close to you. There is an intimacy between you and what you perceive, even if there is a distance at the time. So it is fine to walk over to where it is and fill your frame.

Also, if possible, when filling the frame with the perception, try to have the plane of your camera parallel to the plane of the perception. Partially this helps stabilize the image. "Stop the mind by stopping the eye" is another of our slogans. Also, it helps make sure the image is filled with your flash and not other, accidental information.

To clarify, let's discuss the color assignment. Imagine you are in a parking lot. With closed eyes, you spin around and stop. You open your eyes, and there is a flash of red square on white. You flashed on the corner of a red sign on a white wall across the parking lot. If you made an image from where you are, your image would include the whole sign and the whole wall. But your flash of perception was only part of this scene. So don't make the image from where you are. Walk across the parking lot and fill the frame with the corner of the red sign. The image will be a red square shape in the corner of a white space.

It will not always be a small element like this example. It could be large, like the red curve of a gas station sign against the blue sky. Use the same principle and approach. You are not making an image of a gas sign but of a red curve against a blue background.

This is an exercise. When you actually engage the practice of clear seeing, you don't always have to close your eyes and spin around. The flash of perception just happens. If it is the color assignment, suddenly there will be a flash of color. So it is a matter of recognizing the flash of perception, staying with it and being oriented by it. You can always use this flash of perception exercise to jump-start synchronization or flash of perception while shooting.

The filling the frame with the flash of perception approach is basic to all Nalanda Miksang practice, whether you arrived at that flash on your own, through the synchronization exercise or the flash of perception exercise.

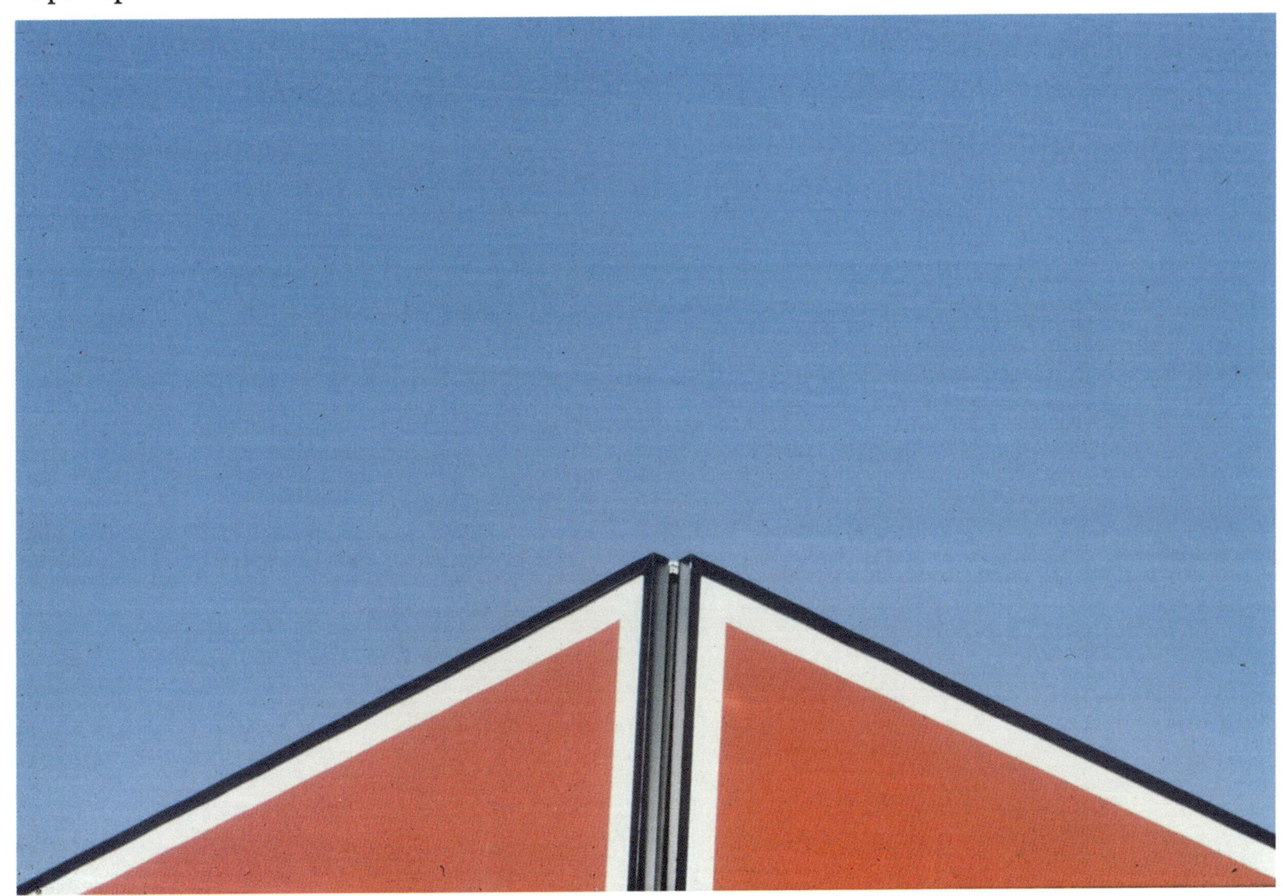

GOING BLIND: A TEACHING TALE FROM JOHN

Imagine you are suddenly blind. You will never recover your eyesight. In practical terms, you have to learn to live again: learn how to walk, make change, and make a cup of tea, so many details. How devastating.

Beyond the logistics of relearning how to get through a day, you mourn the simple fact of vision. You miss things you used to see but didn't even realize you saw: light changing throughout the day and the seasons, the kaleidoscope of colors we daily encounter, openings of space, looking into someone's eyes.

You are forced to realize that vision isn't a fact—it's a miracle. We call this a miracle because it is more or less unconditional. It is sheer manifestation. From the moment most of us open our eyes as infants, we open to this miracle of vision, a gift that keeps on giving. Whether we are male or female, young or old, smart or not so smart, successful or not, rich or poor, most of us are born with this luck.

Yet we do not appreciate vision. We take it for granted. We often live a half-blind life, drifting in a kind of habitual haze, seeing in limited, functional ways to get through an average day in an average way, using what we see in a functional way only—how is the room I just entered arranged, what colors should I wear today, etc. Logistics are ok and a part of how our sight is organized. Despite having this miracle bestowed on us, we tend to live an average life. We just get by. We feel basically ok, but not Basically Good. We doubt our own goodness. We are not living our full potential.

We close the door on this visual feast, trying to nurture ourselves in more obscure ways: through money, entertainment, sleep, etc. Some of us, all of us at some times, would rather live in the self-enclosure of a half-blind world than risk the openness of seeing fully.

So we sense that something is missing in our lives. Something is missing: living complete lives.

The good news is that our life is not really missing. It never can be. Vision regularly reports the visual world. It is just a matter of tuning in to that ordinary miracle, not just seeing in a functional way but really appreciating it. How do we tune in? Just noticing the gaps in our habitual ways, where a beautiful leaf or grimy dumpster really grabs our attention, stops our thought stream, and brings us into the present. This is going on all the time under our blind gazes. While we still have vision, let's really appreciate it.

ASSIGNMENT ONE: COLOR as COLOR

Synchronizing mind and body is also connected with how we synchronize or connect with the world, how we work with the world altogether. This process has two stages that could be called looking and seeing...the point is to look properly. See the colors: white, black blue, yellow, red, green, purple. Look. This is your world! You cannot not look. There is no other world. This is your world: it is your feast. You inherited this, you inherited these eyeballs, you inherited this world of color. Look at the greatness of the whole thing. Look! Don't hesitate. Look! Open your eyes. Don't blink, and look, look - look further.

Then you might see something, which is the second stage. The more you look the more inquisitive you are, the more you are bound to see. Your looking process is not restrained because you are genuine, you are gentle, you have nothing to lose and nothing to fight against..you can see so beautifully. In fact, you can feel the warmth of red and the coolness of blue and the penetrating quality of green - all at once. You appreciate the world around you. It is a fantastic new discovery of the world. You would like to explore the entire universe.

- Chögyam Trunpga Rinpoche, Shambhala Sacred Path of the Warrior

Set aside time, prepare your camera, prepare your schedule, and prepare yourself. Set the intent and structure, and check in with your motivation. If your computer or the laundry calls to you, ask it to call back later. Get out and practice, or stay in and practice; regardless, let yourself into the experience fully. Give yourself a good hour on your first shoot, so you can really sink in and explore.

To open your session, simply walk around, letting yourself naturally connect to the environment. Revisit the descriptions of synchronization and flash of perception exercises. Let the shooting come naturally, and make sure to take breaks to appreciate the world. Don't get stuck behind your camera. Let your whole body enjoy the practice.

Although we work with intent, noticing, looking, and seeing, the main point is that clear seeing is always already available. All these practices are just ways of tuning in to that.

By trusting the magic, we turn our mind into our allies. The playfulness of the phenomenal world is just that: playful. The world is unique and sacred, just like you. To see that you have to be present with the moment, you have to be connected, in sync, harmonized, resonating, aware, and awake. Our birthright is to be connected, aware, and awake. So it turns out that, fundamentally, our mind is not our worst enemy. It is, always was, and always will be our best friend. This is the contemplative view and the contemplative Way.

When you open to a perception or when a flash of perception opens to you, just stay with it. Let it hold your attention—gently. Stay with it, looking and seeing. Let the flash of perception compose your picture for you. After all, the true subject of every Nalanda Miksang photograph is perception, regardless of the assignment. Fill the frame with that flash of perception. Then your image will be an equivalent of that simple and vivid perception. You make an image, let go, and move on. You continue to work with the intent of seeing, recognizing, and working with these openings of perception, these full manifestations of color.

FIRST ASSIGNMENT: COLOR AS COLOR

The first assignment works with the visual element of color.

First, we look at color.

Then, we see (perceive) color.

Finally, we make an image of color.

We start with color because, as a visual phenomenon it is simple, direct, and available. Color naturally attracts our attention. It is easier to make an image of it. For most people, color is visually more prominent than pattern. Texture begins to take us into light, and light requires more attention and craft.

The exercise is to see not only color; the assignment is to see color as color. The assignment is to perceive color as a pure element of the visual world and deliver this through images. The world is full of colorful things, but the assignment is not directed toward colorful things. We notice color that is free from its reference to things, color that is free of any context or constraint, and free of preferences and associations. Color free of outer contexts and inner interpretations. Nondualistic color.

Free-floating color is purely a perception: a perception of color as color—not colorful things. We are breaking with the formation of the thing world. Color as pure perception is color as an expression of the phenomenal world, which is to say, the world of perception.

The slogan for this exercise is "Fire-engine red, not a red fire engine."

Also, more subtly, the assignment is to not see color as a feature of the other the visual elements of level one: not color as space, not color as dot in space, not color as revealed by light, and so forth, though these other visual elements are almost always also in play. (Rarely do we get a shot that is purely a level one assignment. That is ok. Color just needs to be the dominant element.)

Color as color. Just that color. Basic and simple. Here is a series of examples.

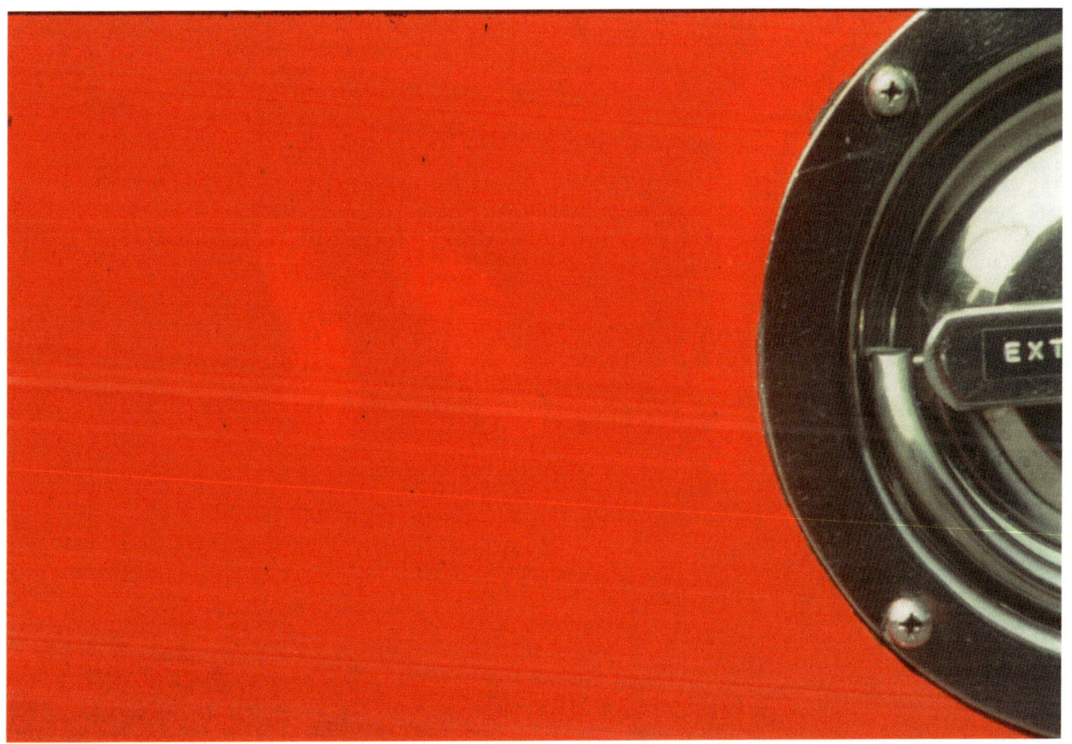
EXT

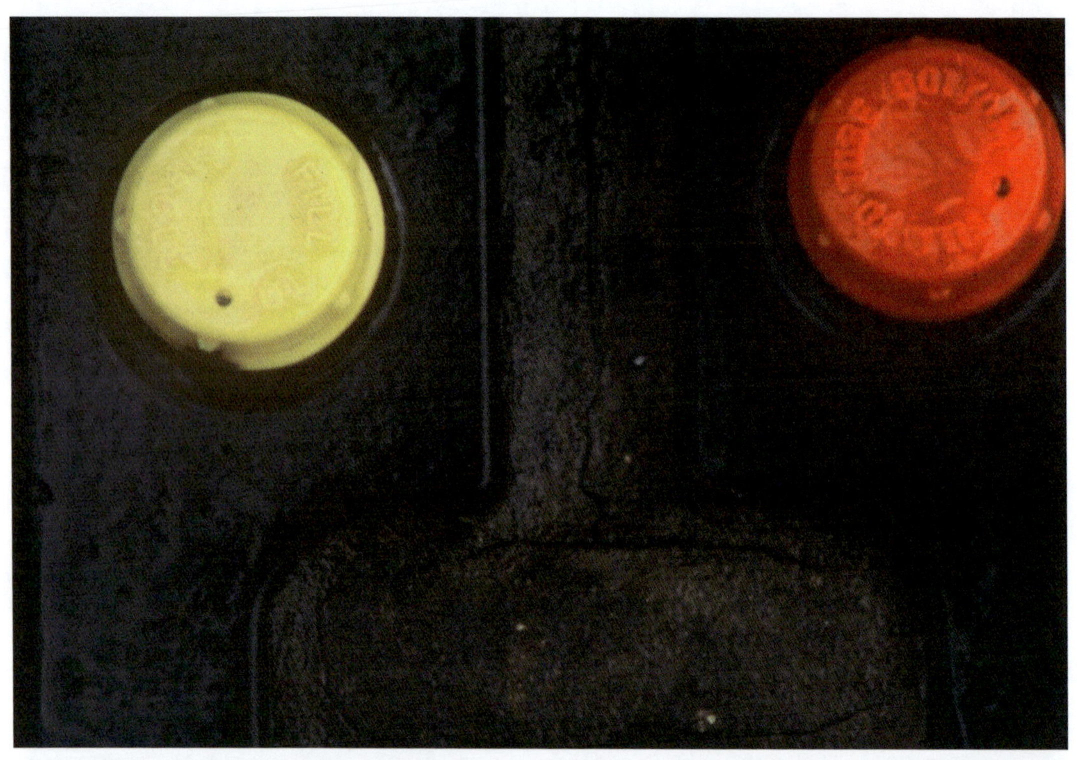

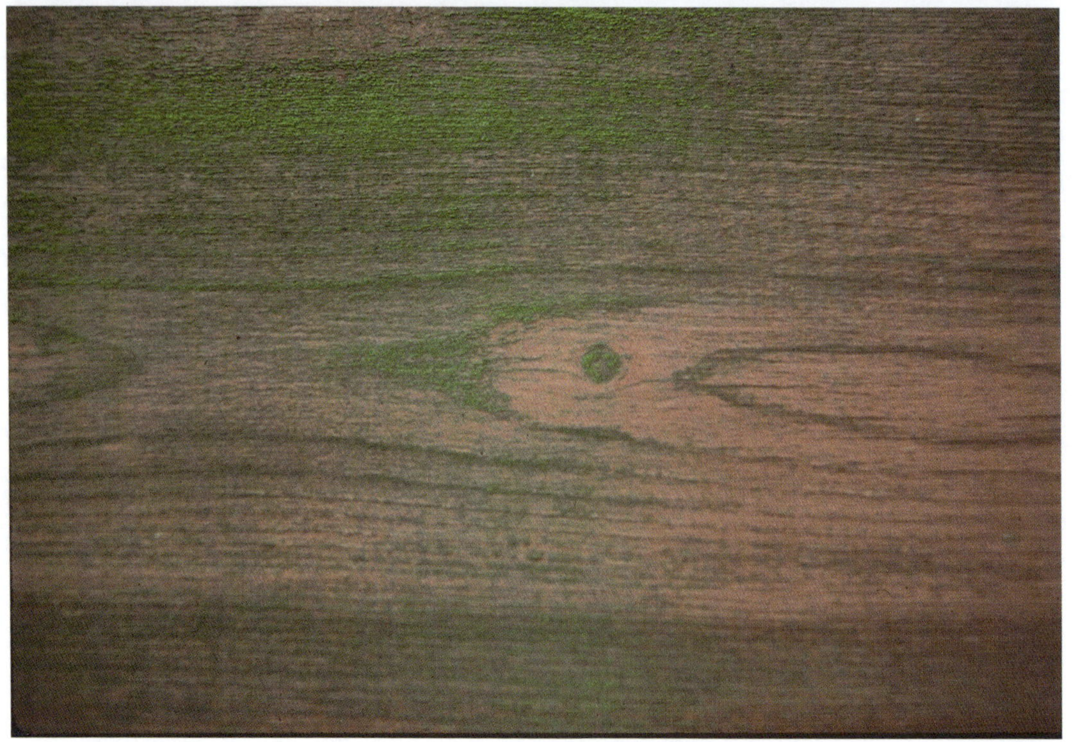

In the examples, you can see many possible color perceptions. Note that all fill the frame with the flash of perception, so there is no more and no less than the pure perception of color. You can see that it need not be just one color, that color can appear as a small but potent part of the image. Lastly, color doesn't have to be a bold primary color (red, blue, yellow); it can be subtle. However, if the color is too subtle, the image comes out less as color and more as texture or space.

FURTHER SUGGESTIONS

At first, it may be difficult to break with seeing colorful things. We want to register color as color. Either or both of the practices of synchronization and flash of perception will help you see just color. Intent, perseverance, and relaxation all help pure color perception manifest.

For your first outings, we recommend that you photograph along a shopping area of a town or city street. Cities manifest endless color: painted doors, multitudes of signs, buildings, cars and trucks, garages and fences in alleyways, fire hydrants, industrial wastelands, store awnings, patio umbrellas, forms in shop windows, etc. If you find major street scenes too distracting, then work in quieter streets, alleyways, or industrial areas.

When we teach the course, we rule out nature as a subject matter for the color shoot. Flowers, and other pieces of nature, tend toward being perceived as flowers, and therefore become pictures of flowers rather than images of color.

For contemplative photography, one of the more difficult subject matters is flowers: they are both too obvious and too subtle to appear as something other than themselves. Eventually we will meet flowers, but for the Color as Color assignment, try working with an urban setting.

We also suggest not taking on people as subjects; again, their energy is strong and something we handle more in level two. For now, keep it simple: color as color. Trust us. There's plenty out there to perceive and photograph.

Finally, the practice is more about process than product. This doesn't mean there isn't craft involved in photographing—there is. But we are coming in through the back door. Let your heart connect with the world, in the structure of the assignment, and photograph from there. Try to only take one shot at a time, and take the same picture only twice. If it doesn't work, move on. Also, aim to take no more than sixty pictures an hour.

ON OBSTACLES

Perhaps you get out there to find you can't take a single picture, much less sixty. Sometimes a session may seem to not go well. You may not feel very synchronized and settled. Maybe you cannot settle down and settle in. Maybe you are anxious about the assignment itself. Somehow no flashes of perception arrive. The whole session feels like a big struggle.

This is not unusual. It is part of the process. Often we try too hard. We try to see clearly. We don't have to try. You may be caught by a subtle, or not-so-subtle, ambition and aggression, such as the desire to make an impressive image. With Nalanda Miksang, you effortlessly make hundreds and thousands of impressive images, so relax about that and enjoy the practice.

A related obstacle is struggling to get the image. Sometimes your equipment is not suitable for taking an image of what you see. That's fine. Let it go and move on. There is no special perception or image to capture—the perceptual world is rich beyond measure. Endless brilliant perceptions provide for endless brilliant images. Indeed, letting go and moving on is itself a contemplative practice.

Remember, you can always go back to synchronization. Give some attention to other aspects of your experience: sensation of walking, smells, or sounds. As you no longer look for them, you notice many colors here and there. When it feels right, if you want, you can make images of the colors that arrive.

Even then, sometimes the obstacles can seem too thick and stifling. If it feels too hard, give yourself a break. Take a break. Nalanda Miksang practice is the opposite of struggle. It is a discipline of relaxation and joy.

Still, sometimes we encounter what Nalanda Miksang calls *dead batteries eye syndrome*. Despite your intent, nothing happens. You walk and walk, you look and look, but you don't see. Or sometimes you see too much: the visual stimulation is overwhelming, and you cannot settle down, settle into the practice. Or you are over thinking or you are feeling too much.

All of these are what Buddhism calls *poverty mind*. We believe we are not good enough or the world isn't good enough. Or we believe there's never enough, or paradoxically, that there's too much, and we don't deserve it. This is a tangled place. It's good to not fight it too much. You can get even more lost. Regardless of where we think the poverty is, we react in one of two ways: over-shoot, trying to consume enough images to feel satisfied, or under-shoot, afraid we can't make it work.

Let go of the struggle; let go of the intent and the exercise. Don't give up, but take a light break. Go for a coffee, a cup of tea, a glass of wine, whatever. If you are doing the exercise with friends, maybe chat or just sit on a bench and watch the comings and goings. Maybe you begin to notice the way the light comes through a glass of water with ice cubes and a lime, or you notice the yellow plastic bag blowing and billowing in the wind through the park—maybe you begin to relax and begin to notice. If so, go back to the session because now you are seeing.

Or not. Some sessions—not many but some—just don't seem to work. Or they are too much work and not enough play. This is the time to develop a sense of humor and a longer sense of the path. It's just one particular session. There will be other lively sessions—very lively. So you can let go. Let go of this particular day. No negative judgment about yourself or the world. Letting go, nonjudgment, nonaggression, a sense of humor—these are also lively characteristics of the contemplative mind.

CLOSING YOUR FIRST SHOOT

Closing is different than ending or stopping. If possible, do not do that. Sometimes for practical reasons, we have to stop or end a shoot without closing. If possible, do this in the contemplative way of closing.

We can't tell you when it is time to close. This will vary from shoot to shoot and from person to person. It is personal and measured by you, as you are, in the shoot, being the shoot. Becoming more familiar with yourself as a contemplative photographer will help you will recognize the sense of enough, such as a slight drop of intensity.

When it is time to put away your camera, it is not the end of the shoot. It is the beginning of closing. You continue to look and see. You drop the intent of the particular assignment—in this case, Color as Color—and continue to see in an open and clear way, riding the wave of synchronization, illuminated by the lightning flashes of perception.

At this point, it is important that you do not give in to the temptation to take out your camera and make more images. This temptation will be intense since suddenly, you see so much that is fantastic! Don't forget: there is no single special perception and no single special image. Try to recall that what is unique is you and this phenomenal world together: just now/just that/just so. Just look and see, and enjoy the amazing open, detailed, and vivid play and display of the phenomenal world.

This closing in the contemplative manner is also a bridge to an opening. It is a conduit to practice Nalanda Miksang by appreciating the amazing, open, detailed, and vivid play and display of the phenomenal world throughout your day-to-day life. This is the real Nalanda Miksang. This is the real contemplative life.

CONTINUOUS PRACTICE

Throughout the week, you can continue to practice without formally practicing. Recall that clear seeing and the flash of perception are natural to being human. Throughout the day and the week, just tune in to color. Or just tune in to clear seeing and visual appreciation. This is wakeful and joyful. Punctuate the tendency to gloss over things and slip into the habitual blur of the nondescript life.

Of course, the tasks of our everyday life call to us. However, to live daily life, we need not be unaware. Color does not care about your personal state of mind. Color and the perceptual phenomenal world only radiate. They radiate reality, and that is good. We are always already connected, which we can discover if we let ourselves relax.

You can also do spot shooting throughout the week. No one said practice has to be only a long, single shoot. Keep your camera available. You can make images as the perceptions appear. See the way light plays on the bedroom wall late in the day. It is enough to see this, but you can also make an image. Doing so occasionally helps keep the intention of clear seeing lively and continuous.

Or you can have little sessions, whatever and whenever—take your camera with you when you walk to the corner store and back.

Be careful with this way of practicing. It can become an issue if you find that you are always shooting. If you are always carrying your camera and capturing images—even of your friend who comes for a visit—then you are moving away from the contemplative intent. This is something that Chogyam Trungpa called *spiritual materialism*: you are now turning the contemplative practice into a grasping, material practice. It comes from poverty mind. This is poison. If you find yourself doing this, try to return to looking and seeing—without photographing.

Stay loose and free. Stay alert and at ease. Just trust the everyday magic.

PERSONAL STORY: JOHN

I vividly recall my first outing with the color exercise. I encountered the flash of perception then. It was the summer of 1983. It was a bright, hot summer day, and I went to Lakefield, a small village in Southern Ontario. I entered the village with the intent to see color. It was difficult. I saw lots of colorful things and lots of colors. I even took a few photographs, but somehow I knew that wasn't it. I looked and looked, and walked and walked. Nothing was happening. My growing sense of frustration became a struggle. All kinds of thoughts and anxieties crowded in: *I can't get it*; *I won't have anything to show*; *I am running out of time.* I was sweating everywhere; it was hot outside and hotter on the inside, in my mind. Of course, the more I struggled, the less I relaxed. Finally I took a break. At a corner store, I got a cold drink. I left the store, stepped outside, and bang! A dot of white on green across the street. It was a white wood building with a cut-out heart shape in the middle of a green shutter. But all I saw was white dot on green.

Knowing the craft for forming an equivalent image, I walked across the street, filled the viewfinder frame with the white-dot-on-green space, took a meter reading, made the appropriate camera adjustments, and clicked the shutter. I turned away, and bang! A gold filigree pattern on a blue background: the corner of a Royal Bank sign. Then it was bang, bang, bang: color, color, color, all down the street that day—and for the rest of my life since then.

VIEWING THE IMAGES

In the cultural traditions of contemplative practice, whether in artistic or community contexts, viewing has always been a key way to the contemplative mind

For example, many Japanese traditions involve contemplative viewing: annual ventures to see cherry blossoms, moon viewing, snow viewing, firefly viewing, the viewing of sacred and poetic sites, the act of viewing contemplative art manifestations such as rock gardens, and so forth. These occasions engage the ordinary magic of life, culture, and community. As such, they create a contemplative culture.

In the same way, viewing Nalanda Miksang images is not just a learning tool; it is a contemplative community practice.

First of all, as direct feedback, it shows you, and everyone, how you are doing in terms of clear perception and delivering an equivalent image. It is not just feedback about assignment; it is a mirror of your mind. Your mind is projected for the participants and teacher to see. Many beginners find this an anxious occasion. But no personal judgment is made during the viewing, so you can relax. Let it become a celebration of your unique offering to a collective visual feast.

Regarding each image as an intentional perception of the assignment, the teacher or other viewer relates to the student as an intentional perceiver, a practitioner. More deeply, review is the mixing of eyes and minds, that of the teacher and student.

Ideally, as you complete these assignments, you'll participate in the review of your images in a group. Having the support of others in this process is essential, whether this happens online, in your town, or with friends who have also read the book. (You'll find online resources for meeting other practitioners all over the world in the appendices.)

I never attended art school, but I have participated in many writing workshops. I am well aware that criticism can be toxic—intentionally or not—for the person receiving it. Lots of us are afraid of what others will say about our work. The photography world in particular has a bad reputation for being hypercritical.

In Nalanda Miksang, the aim of the review is to synchronize further. I always make sure to let students know that this is not a time to criticize. We are all invested in clear seeing; we are all curious and open. We want to see if the person was able to make an equivalent of an image that prompts us all to experience a similar, if not the same, flash of perception. We are less concerned about if it is a "good shot."

After her first level one, a student told me she was an art school dropout. The major reason she hadn't completed art school was the brutal critiques. Others seemed to feel a piece of art was correctly seen only if they could come up with something wrong about it. I nodded, mentioning my similar experience with writing workshops. In our culture overall, criticism seems to be interpreted as the only intelligence.

Then she went on to cry a little, smiled, and told me this was the first time in her life that she really felt seen—that the participants and I had seen what she saw. I had delivered the news, so to speak, that she *had* missed the shot so gently that it almost seemed like she hadn't done anything wrong.

"But you didn't do anything wrong. You perceived correctly. The shot just didn't happen. You'll figure it out," I replied.

She cried a little further, still smiling. "You mean there's nothing wrong with me?"

I smiled. Here's what we are all so deeply worried about, what we are always waiting to hear, and what so many of us experience as a part of negative critique sessions.

"No. And I am sure this practice can help prove to you that there is nothing wrong with you."

"It already has," she said.

This should be the mentality behind any review, whether it is by you, online, or with others—kindness, accommodation, accuracy, curiosity, and a celebration of the human spirit, senses, and perception. May this one day be the spirit behind all art critiques!

COMMUNITY OF VIEWING

Nalanda Miksang works best as a group practice, with others who have done the assignment.

This has several benefits. First, you can all help each other in truly seeing the images. It provides more insight.

Second, it opens up the collective contemplative imagination. To see how others see is surprising and fresh. How amazingly different people can see—even when doing the same assignment, in the same setting. It is a delight and celebration, to boot, to witness these fresh images of what seems a brand-new world!

Finally, it is deeply contemplative. As a group, you mix eyes, minds, and hearts. You enter the deeply contemplative practice of viewing. Forming community like this is a foundation for entering the Nalanda Miksang society—you join with a larger group intention to bring the goodness of the world to the world. So though it seems a small occurrence to get together and view images, you participate in a big event—the wave and the ocean all at once.

HOW TO REVIEW IMAGES

After you have set up a way for all the viewers to see images, the review can begin. When an image appears on a screen, this is synchronized seeing or a flash of perception all over again. The review is just as much a part of the practice as photographing.

As a viewer, ask yourself: How does the image appear to your eye and mind? Are you seeing the image in the same way the perception showed up for the photographer? In terms of this particular assignment, is it color as color? Do you experience a direct, full sense of color?

Viewing this way is much like viewing the phenomenal world: it is open, fresh, and direct. Yet for the review, its time to add some of what Buddhism calls *discernment*. Use your own direct experience of shooting to sense, from your own eyes, whether the image on the screen is color as color. If the image works, the image is an equivalent of that perception. Bang! The image stops the eye and stops the mind.

If the image doesn't quite work, two things remain to figure out: What was the original perception? Does the image offer an image of this perception?

Sometimes the image itself isn't an equivalent of the perception, but you can see the original perception in the image. It may be hidden. Maybe too many other things are going on. If the images are yours, perhaps you remember. You can ask if it belongs to someone else. If you can't find the original perception in the image, ask yourself: Is this a Nalanda Miksang image?

Maybe it is an object that *has* color. Maybe it's a purple chair against a red background. Or perhaps the color is part of a design. Maybe it looks like a piece of abstract art, too interesting to be just a color as color shot. These are two examples of *color plus*: more than the direct simplicity of color as color.

These are still Nalanda Miksang images. They have the quality and characteristics of Nalanda Miksang images: authentic presence, simplicity, directness, space, and purity. They just don't belong to this particular assignment. In the first case, the image is of color as part of a larger level two perception of ordinary world. In the second, it is color as abstract art, what we call *Absolute Eye*.

Without these other assignments under your belt, these first reviews can be a bit tricky. Don't worry too much about categories of what the image is if it isn't color as color. Just be aware that you can capture many clear perceptions out on this first shoot that are not color as color. The more you learn, the more you'll be able to discern what makes a clear photograph from a clear perception and what doesn't. This is why this is an ongoing training – less focused on labels than experience, while labels still help us to clarify.

And since you have not yet tried the other assignments or levels, how are you having these other perceptions and making their equivalent images? Most likely because you have opened to clear seeing and pure perception. The flash of perception opens perception itself. It does not know about the Nalanda Miksang assignments.

Instead, the assignments channel open perception and shape it into a contemplative path. The neutral flash of perception sometimes shows up in ways other than the particular assignment. In the review, you simply note that it is Nalanda Miksang, just not part of this particular assignment.

Finally, the images may not be Nalanda Miksang at all. You may have fallen back into conventional, conceptual ways of seeing and making images. They may be documentary: representations of the thing world. They may be artistic constructions, heavy on photographic technique. Then, simply acknowledge this and move on.

Regardless of whether they are Nalanda Miksang images or not, the photographs may have craft issues: they may be out of focus or not exposed properly. Craft is important. Craft has a contemplative dimension. At this stage, we do not emphasize craft. At this stage in the training, we emphasize the primacy of perception: the contact with direct perception through clear seeing.[1]

Most craft issues self-correct through practice. Craft requirements in this practice are minimal. It is not difficult to learn these basics.

Another contemplative issue with craft is that sometimes you may try to make your camera do something it can't do. Maybe you shoot something too close or too far away, or at an angle you can't capture with your lens. If so, then let go and move on. A single best perception or image doesn't exist. Letting go and moving on is part of contemplative practice.

PERCEPTUAL FOCUS

Sometimes the image reveals clear and direct perception, but the perception it shows is not a single one. This issue is key to delivering a Nalanda Miksang image.

This often happens when you first practice Nalanda Miksang. Such images bear a trace of the flash of perception that was the focus of the clear seeing. However, the resulting image includes too much other information. The simplicity of the direct perception becomes lost in the complicated image.

---

1 Please see our appendix for suggestions on contemplative camera craft.

Because Nalanda Miksang images are simple, spacious, and pure, it doesn't take much for us to notice when they have gotten too complex.

So figure out where the flash of perception is. Teachers often say things like, "The flash of perception seems to be more here, but you have included too much other information." We always ask the photographer what she perceived. Note that this is not the same as what she saw—what we see is often a combination of many perceptions. This puts the emphasis on synchronization versus just taking nice pictures.

Try simplifying the image back to the flash—crop out the extraneous information. Using perceptual framing appropriate to the original perception, you can discover the equivalent image—simple, direct, and strong. Looking freshly again at the cropped image will reveal the definite and composed feeling of the original flash. Cropping is used to deliver afresh, with no distractions, the actual image the person perceived. However, this only works if the framing helps reveal it. If it doesn't match the photographer's perception—even if it makes a nice or interesting photo—then we've left the practice of contemplative viewing behind.

In the image review, we learn to discern flashes of perception. This helps all of the viewers to feel what it is like when images deliver equivalents of flashes—that focal singularity, just that, just so. Cropping helps us experience when it works and when it doesn't. This is a direct way to improve our shooting. There's no need to memorize rules.

Finally there is the 10 percent craft issue. This is a physical property of most cameras. Digital images usually include 10 percent more content along the outside edges than what is in the viewfinder or LCD screen, so the image contains more information than the original flash of perception. The result is, at minimum a distraction, and perceptual impact is decreased.

Recall that the way of Nalanda Miksang is to stop the mind by stopping the eye. This unintended extra content can pull viewers' eyes away from the flash. It is as if the image is like a balloon that has a pinprick and is deflating. Instead of a taut, buoyant manifestation, it loses air. In simple images like these, a tiny distraction magnifies.

Here's how to crop out the extra 10 percent while you are shooting: simply move a half step closer, and then refocus. This can feel awkward at first, but it will soon become second nature and you will deliver your actual flash of perception.

Pay relaxed attention to what happens. Gently hold the final image in mind while you are composing with the camera. Immediately, the image becomes strong visually and perceptually: it stops the eye and stops the mind. It becomes an equivalent image.

PERSONAL STORY: JOHN

I recall an incident from a couple decades ago. My colleague Michael Wood and I were teaching Miksang for the Naropa Institute summer program in Halifax, Nova Scotia. In those days—and to some extent still to this day—central Halifax was visually monochromatic: the buildings were made of gray or brown limestone. In the color review, one student showed an image of a street view of downtown Halifax. I immediately thought, *This is a miss.*

But Michael stayed with it. After some contemplation, he said, "It's the red mailbox right?"

Say what? What red mailbox?

Sure enough, in the distance was a little red dot. That was the *perceptual action*—what the student perceived—but she did not make the equivalent image. She did not fill the frame with the flash of perception. The perception was accurate: red as red. But to deliver the equivalent image, she still had to cross the physical space to deliver the visual perception—to fill the frame with the red of that red mailbox. Just that red, just so.

MORE ON IMAGES

Sometimes practitioners ask, "Why do we need to make images? If the point is clear seeing, why don't we just go out and look?" Why not, indeed!

Isn't the perfect meditation instruction "Just be"?

So why do we need to, for many hours and many years, focus on such practices as sitting, focusing attention, visualizations, and so forth? Why can't we just be?

We cannot because of the momentum of our habitual tendencies. We want to *not* "just be." We are driven by our desires, confusion, and habitual modes of being, and confused by our tangle of concepts, opinions, and conventional views. As Plato intuited, we live in a dimly lit cave. We are fascinated only by the play of shadows on the wall.

Chögyam Trungpa frequently uses the image of a cocoon to describe how we shut ourselves off from the world in fear and confusion. But the sun is shining in the open, beyond the confines of this self-absorbed cocoon. Clear seeing is our natural condition. What can leverage us free of the momentum of habitual distraction? What can help reconnect with our basic sense of wholesomeness?

It is like sailing. You use the wind to sail against the wind, by tacking and zigzagging back and forth. Sometimes the wind fills your sails, and it is a joyous adventure. Sometimes, it's just plain struggle. Regardless, you need the sails. Without them, you're dead in the water, aimlessly drifting at the caprice of currents.

It is the same with clear seeing. We have to claim our birthright, use our capacity to really see. Practicing contemplative photography is a kind of sail, steering us back to the ordinary magic of clear seeing. Making an image is using that sail to catch the joy of the world.

First, the intention of making an image helps focus our clear seeing. It directs us into a path of training. Otherwise, our attempts will likely be superficial, and easily distracted and diffused. Here's a paradox of the contemplative and meditative approaches: it takes some discipline to be at ease.

Finally, the images are beautiful, especially when you enter level two and beyond. Sometimes, they are even art. Bringing further beauty into the world is intrinsically good. It enriches our culture. No wonder images are so appreciated in the Nalanda Miksang community.

NONATTACHMENT

The real impact of the contemplative practice is lost when you get attached to images or to your ambition to create great images. Just relax. Nalanda Miksang is an image machine. Enter the Way, become the Way, and you start making thousands upon thousands of brilliant images without even trying.

Here is a nonattachment contemplation: What happens to this pile of brilliant images? At best, few see the light of day as prints. At best, some are presented in shows. At best, some find the light of a computer screen. And the thousands of others? They are destined to spend their existence in the void of digital darkness.

So don't get too attached. Rather, appreciate each brilliant image on the occasion of its birth. Be present for the whole moment. Don't get vacation syndrome: don't remember only what you saw through the camera lens. Stay with now. This is a mirror of your brilliant manifestation.

CREATIVE UNIVERSE

How, during the format of a weekend workshop, do most participants create at least a few masterpiece images? Often these are as strong and beautiful as works by acknowledged masters of photographic art.

How is that possible? How is it possible that someone may have little knowledge of photography and only a beginning discipline of clear seeing, yet nevertheless create a masterpiece image?

The secret is that you don't create the image. As senior Nalanda Miksang teacher Maxine Sidran puts it, "In Nalanda Miksang, we find a way to let the universe make an image of itself."

This is the deep source of contemplative creativity: the creative universe itself. In large measure, the practice of contemplative photography is to get you out of the way so that you can enter the Way. No matter how smart, accomplished, or creative you may be, you can never be more creative than creation itself. So let creation create: that is as good as it gets.

This is not mysticism. It works. It shows up in the joy of the process and in all the images—not only the masterpiece images, but in all the images themselves.

COMPLETING COLOR

Viewing your images and those of others completes an assignment. You may learn something new about composing an image. That is good. But the image is much more than composition.

One of the hallmarks and secrets of contemplative photography is that the heart of the composition is already there as pure perception. Always. Each pure perception manifests with its inherent focal point and its appropriate perceptual framing. Making an image is guided by this natural perceptual composition as much as possible. Filling the frame with the clear perception is an example of this.

In viewing and reviewing, the image is seen clearly and corrected, so it can fully deliver an equivalent of its inherent perceptual composition.

This is the way of contemplative composition—view an image the same way you connect with a flash of perception.

Nalanda Miksang images are strong, vivid, and joyful. This is what the image transmits. This is what pure perception communicates.

Direct perception stops the eye and stops the mind. When the eye is held, the mind is held. When the mind is held, it is still and composed. It is gathered, alert, and reflective. It identifies with what it sees—that's interesting, that's fantastic, that's beautiful. That's *that*.

Reverberating through the many dimensions of direct perception, aesthetic emotion and visceral insight is vivid appreciation. This is the Way of Seeing.

REPEATING COLOR

Each of these assignments is truly endless and never done.

Once you have completed the process of the assignment, it is a good time to repeat the assignment and the process. Image review gives you a better sense of how it went and how it can go, a sense of how some of your attempts miss the point and how some are on target. A few are bull's eyes: pure synchronized eye and mind, a pure image equivalent.

Having had this experience and insight, you can practice the process a second time in a more informed and focused way. Start with intention, head through perception, make images, and review images again. The more you practice, the more you can relax. You enter the process with more ease and depth, developing confidence in the Way of pure perception as the Way of contemplative photography. You are on your way as a contemplative.

TWO SIDE EXERCISES

We include here two supplementary exercises that don't fit into the regular weekend format of a Nalanda Miksang program. These are lovely exercises. They can be done anytime in the process of studying and practicing Nalanda Miksang. They are not about a particular assignment so much as taking on a different way of shooting.

We offer them here because they also help show all the ways we can see differently or are already doing so if we just stop to notice and photograph. These exercises encourage you to go beyond your personal perceptual limits, even your contemplative perceptual limits.

MULTIPLE IMAGE EXERCISE

With the synchronization and flash of perception approach, we usually start with a specific assignment. Then, we move on to the next in a series. With this exercise, we encourage you to go further and into more detail. Here, you explore the same subject in a different perceptual way, making multiple images of separate flashes of perception.

For this exercise, choose a nondescript subject matter. It needs to be a perceptual challenge. An appropriate subject matter will be not too big or too small. A house or car is too big. A wallet might be too small. It will work best if the object is nondescript, something very ordinary and mundane. An example of the combination of the right size and mundane-ness would be a standard metal garbage bin, a Dumpster from the back alley of a business.

Regardless of your object, the assignment is to explore it in a perceptual way. You can set up whatever seem the appropriate parameters: a ten-shot exploration, a twenty-shot exploration, etc. Make it at least ten.

Two key points to remember:

1. **This is a perceptual exploration.** You break with the subject matter as a thing. You open to all the in-the-moment perceptual details: color, texture, etc.

2. **Limit you exploration of any one particular perception.** Don't just repeat ten or twenty shots of the same perception. Move on to other flashes. We always suggest limiting your attempts to take an image. Here, repeat up to two or three times, then move on. Really let yourself explore all aspects including the assignments we have done so far.

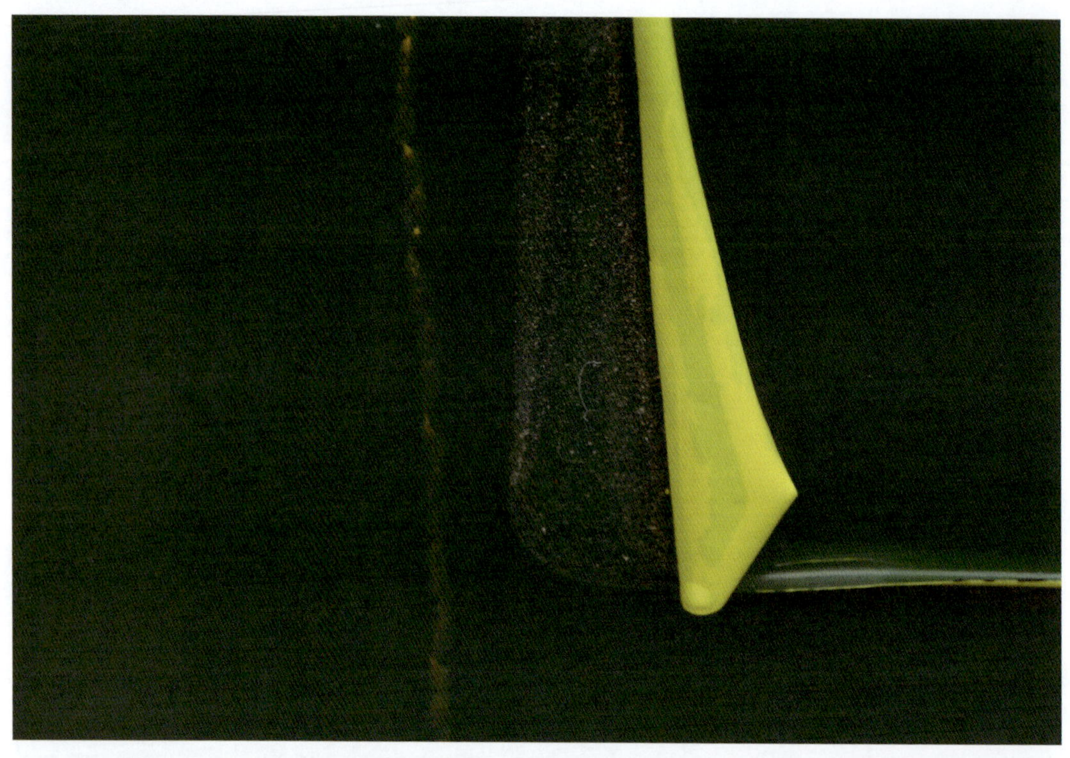

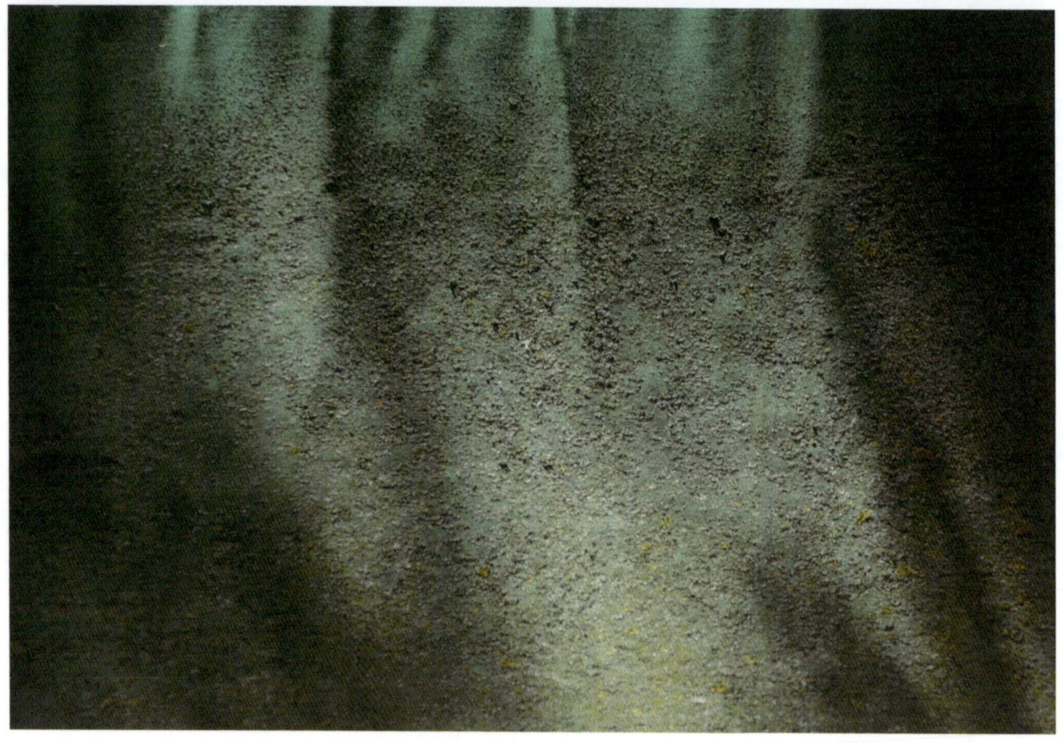

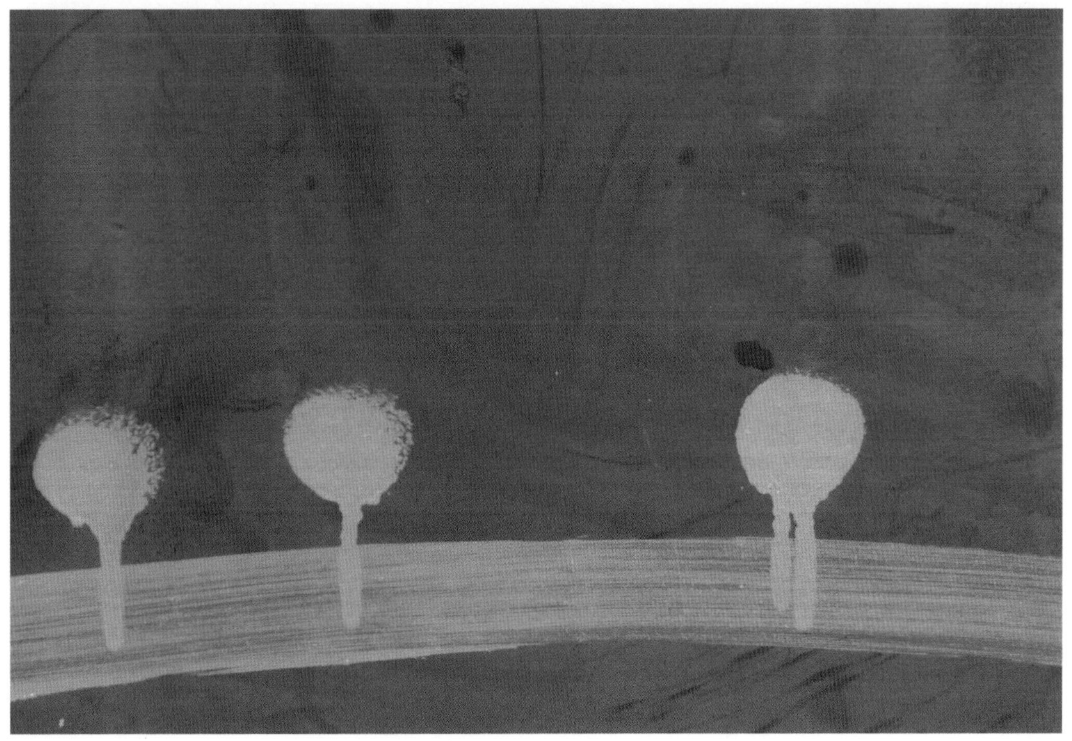

In my early days, for this exercise, my colleague Michael Wood assigned other participants workable subject matters: mailboxes, a wall, so forth. Because I was a Miksang teacher, he gave me a slightly more challenging exercise: I had to shoot a gray concrete light post, an almost impossible subject for making images conventionally.

As it turns out, this object had a lot of perceptual possibility. I found my way through the Way of perception: I noticed nuts and bolts, the edge of the pole against the asphalt, the dot of the lamp against the vast blue sky, the curve of the shape, etc. Perception opened this object to me, because a light post is a manifestation of pure openness.

In another example, I explored a green industrial Dumpster. Though at first it seemed an impossible subject, soon I noticed chips in the topcoat of green paint. In previous incarnations, it had been painted in different colors. These openings revealed those colors. I could have easily made ten images of these color chips. But that was not the point, so I moved on to other aspects, like texture.

Even still, more and more I was challenged. I came to   an impasse. It seemed there was nothing more to see. Being patient with the impasse, I finally felt a release, something else opened—something new and more detailed.

But after nine shots, I was desperate again. *There's nothing more to see without repeating*, I thought. In desperation, I climbed on top of the bin where there were little pools of water from the evening rain.

The phenomenal world is so generous if we just go along on the adventure it offers.

PERCEPTUAL GAZE EXERCISE

This is a similar exercise. It is an exercise in the practice of looking. In looking as looking, see what you see before any concept arises. You don't even need your camera for this. Just look at something very basic and simple, like a simple dining room chair.

What do you see? What does your eye see? A dining room chair? Something else? What does it actually see in terms of visual phenomena? Shape and color, perhaps texture. We often see gradients. Shapes and colors are seldom blatant; they are detailed, blended, and subtle. It depends on the light and so forth. That is actual visual manifestation—what your eye sees.

In practical terms (sitting on something) and concept (labeling/naming), we call this phenomenal manifestation, this thing, "a dining room chair." To be clear, there's nothing wrong with this. Concepts and labels are part of how we find our way.

But this is not our whole experiential world, a world we often reduce to useful concepts. Life lived this way is a limited life. This exercise is designed to open up the plenitude of the phenomenal world beyond our everyday conceptual limitations.

After contemplating your perceptions of something simple like a chair, look—*really* look—at a more multidimensional situation, for example, the offering water bowls on a Buddhist shrine.

What do you see? Offering bowls? No. Before and beyond "offering bowls," see the many expressions of light, color, reflection, refraction, etc.

Look and see. See what you see—the multifaceted visual phenomenal world.

SECTION FOUR:

VIEW INTERLUDE

Your own wisdom as a human being is not separate from the power of things as they are. They are both reflections of an unconditioned wisdom...Therefore, there is no fundamental separation between you and your world. When you experience these two things together as one, so to speak, then you have access to tremendous vision and power in the world—you find that they are inherently connected to your own vision, your own being. That is discovering magic.

—Chögyam Trungpa, *Shambhala Sacred Path of the Warr*

SIGHT AND INSIGHT

Now you have begun the basics of Nalanda Miksang contemplative photography. You have a general presentation of the view, and the first assignment: Color as Color. You have also begun to learn how to do all the assignments and explore all the elements of the visual world.

Your next assignment will to explore light.

Before light, let's pause and consider more about view. Remember, the contemplative Way soars with the wings of view and practice. If you feel inspired and excited to shoot, you can skip this section for now and move on to light. Then come back to these contemplations when you are satiated with direct experience and a multitude of beautiful images.

THREE LEVELS OF PERCEPTION

Nalanda Miksang is based in visual perception. What we mean by perception is our interaction with the world through our senses. In the case of Miksang, through our visual or sight organ. In general, perception is that facility that connects the inner with the outer.

Deep down, many of us believe that there is a perceiver (e.g., a human being) and something perceived (e.g., a maple leaf). We think that the human and the leaf are separate: we hold a deep conviction that there is someone who sees this other thing. We think of them, as if the perceiver and perceived are at opposite ends of a long pole from one another spectrum. It is correct that there is *seeing*, but the idea of a separate perceiver and perceived is wrong.

Dharma teachings say that this separation is fundamentally inaccurate. There is no substantial separation between the perceiver and the perceived. They are not-one, and they are also not-two.

The practice of Nalanda Miksang is to purify the relationship between the perceiver and the perceived so that there is less sense of being separate, so we can really begin to sense a dynamic reciprocity between the world and ourselves. When the perceiver and perceived are harmonized, there is a sense of fulfillment, joy, peace, and magic. This connects us to the phenomenal world—though we are always connected, our wrong view keeps us feeling separate.

Western phenomenology focuses on this separation and says we can never attain a true connection between perceiver and perceived. According to Buddhist teachings, this place and state of pure connection does exist. It is called the phenomenal world.

This Buddhist path of phenomenology has three levels, or stages. They are based on a Chögyam Trungpa's dharma art teaching the Three Levels of Perception. Overall, these three levels of perception offer a path of transformation through clear seeing. The first level works is recognizing clear seeing, the second level explores the aesthetics of that clear seeing, and the third level presents the direct manifestation of that clear seeing.

In Nalanda Miksang, the three levels are Looking and Seeing, Fields of Perception, and Orderly Chaos. This book presents Looking and Seeing (level one). This first volume is both instruction for the level one teachings, and also an overall introduction to the Way of Seeing.

The primary question of level one is: What is the visual?

Isn't the visual everything we see? Sort of, but it'd be more accurate to say that the visual world is an ongoing manifestation, detailed with richness and unaccountable generosity. But this answer provides no practice, no structure for us to experientially explore. Nalanda Miksang draws on the endless richness and generosity of the visual world, but also includes skillful means, a path, to experience this overwhelming gift.

Nalanda Miksang teaches that the visual world has a structure. Its elements include color, light, surface (a combination of texture and pattern), space, and what we call dot in space.

Try it out. In your field of vision do you find these elements? Is there color? Do you see light? Does your seeing stop at a surface? Does that surface have texture or pattern? Is space a part of your way of seeing? Finally, are there dots in your space? In other words, do you see things—a chair, a cup, a door, a tree, a wall, a person, a cloud?

These visual elements are the focus of level one. We deconstruct the visual world into these basic elements so we can establish a direct and pure relationship with each element. This is the first stage of training: direct visual contact for entering the path of purification.

EXPERIENCE AND THE THREE LEVELS OF PERCEPTION

The Three Levels of Perception teaching helps clarify your practice. It transforms experience into insight.

However, actual experience does not necessarily follow a simple threefold path. Although in level one, we explore the visual elements, in experience, these visual elements do not always appear in the form of a level one assignment. Sometimes they appear as a level two or even a level three photograph. For example, a level one exploration of light would be simply to see and then photograph light as light, say a patch of light on a wall. Simple and direct. But this easily becomes a photograph of a vase, for instance, with a patch of light on it. At that point, the photograph has gone more from being "about the patch of light" to being "about the vase which has a patch of light on it." And then, in level three, perhaps the patch of light expands out and becomes a part of a chaotic energetic space. The line between these three photographs can be quite thin.

But we need structure. So this first volume introduces mostly level one, the practice of clear seeing, and works with the elements of the visual. To some extent this first level is training in visual sensibility, like learning chords and scales in music training. However, it will naturally overlap with level two, especially once we get to the light assignment. So when we present the light assignment, we offer it both in a level one and a level two ways.

Be attentive to the interplay between the three levels view and your actual experience of the visual elements and the visual world.

In Nalanda Miksang, the joining of view and experience produces a subtler and deeper practice. This is the bridge into the way things are. This, in turn, bridges your wisdom with the wisdom of the phenomenal world. In level one, direct contact with pure visual experience awakens you to the dynamic of visual imagery and the vividness of images. This, in turn, introduces you to the inner practice of Nalanda Miksang, level two, which is ultimately a contemplative transformation.

Seeing has two aspects: sight and insight. Nalanda Miksang trains in clear seeing, but also in turning clear seeing into insight. For this deeper contemplation, it is not enough to make brilliant images. It is not even enough to discover and experience fresh seeing. (But if these are your intentions, they are plenty. They will enhance and enrich your life.)

The deeper issue is that experiences, even profound ones, come and go. That's the nature of experience—all experiences, not just yours. The clouds in the sky change. They obey large-scale weather patterns over which we have no control. Like weather, our minds—which we *seem* to have more control over—change constantly. Really understanding this fact is insight.

If your intent is to enter deeply into the meaning and possibility of your life, then you must go deeper. This is when you truly enter the Way of Seeing. You start with the experience of seeing; then, through insight, you gather the wisdom in that experience. We join the word *experience* with the word *wisdom* when we say that someone "is experienced." In other words, she has traveled the path of her life and gathered wisdom through that journey. She is seasoned.

Insight transforms you. Your sight is transformed into wisdom. Recall the key quote from Chögyam Trungpa telling us that our wisdom and the wisdom of the universe are the same unconditioned wisdom.

INTENTION AND REALIZATION

If your intention is to have a good experience and to make brilliant images, that is completely fine—more than fine, it is necessary. It is ground zero of Nalanda Miksang practice. The basic Nalanda Miksang intention is to engage direct perception and make an equivalent image. In Nalanda Miksang, this happens naturally. Having fresh and good experiences, we make brilliant contemplative images.

But you can go deeper. When you do, your intention and realization can become the way of liberation. With practice, you begin to realize there is more than direct experience and making images. You begin to tune in to the results of direct experience: harmonization and joy.

See if these teachings mesh with your own experience as you practice. For instance, something catches your eye, and now you are in suspended contemplative time—the timeless time of the now moment. It is complete. You are there with the *there*. It is just this color as just this color. It is direct and definite.

The mind side of this synchronization event also feels good. It not only feels good, but it also feels electric. Along with peace, you may also feel an edge. Feeling that edge is feeling alive. Is something like this how you feel? Does something like this resonate with your practice, experience, and insight?

The only way to test it out for yourself is to move beyond the experience to insight. Nalanda Miksang is not a dogma. We do not present a belief system. We present a way: a Way of seeing. The paradox is that you *are* the way. Via how you feel, you sense the phenomenal world. How could it be otherwise? It already is. Be yourself, and tune in to that as best you can.

Again, you and the phenomenal world are there together. Which comes first? Does it matter? You are connected. In this creative situation, create. Enjoy.

On a deeper level, your good experience becomes a connection with basic goodness and insight into the ways of things as they are—insight into the Way. Practice is the same as daily living. First, open to the ongoing freshness of life. Then, open to the ongoing basic connection with being alive. Your wisdom touches the wisdom of the phenomenal world, which is an unconditioned primordial wisdom: basic goodness.

Many years ago, Michael Wood offered a Miksang training workshop when he moved to Halifax, Nova Scotia. He invited me to help with the workshop. He had a difficult student, someone who resisted and complained. Michael is a nice guy; he has a teddy-bear quality. I, on the other hand, while being a nice guy, do not have a teddy-bear quality. Students—in particular, Nalanda Miksang teachers—report a certain edge when I review their work.

During the review of the color assignment, this student began a stream of complaints and excuses. My response was, "Color does not care about your state of mind."

This may seem harsh and direct. It is. Not that I was harsh, but rather color as color is direct. There is no room for interpretation or flimflam. Color as color cuts through interpretations and self-absorption, straight to things as they are. It has an edge. There is no cocoon nonsense: there is just sense and sensibility.

But color also offers itself unbiased, endlessly, as color. This is the affirmative point, the positive form of directness.

OUTER, INNER, AND SECRET TEACHINGS

Dharma practices are sometimes presented in terms of outer, inner, and secret teachings. There is not a strict separation of these three spheres of teachings; they overlap. The view helps you orient yourself in this threefold path. To some extent, these three spheres of teaching are ways of joining intention and realization.

So far, we have been concerned with making images. These are the *outer teachings* of Nalanda Miksang. Nalanda Miksang is a practice of clear seeing. We move from conventional ways of seeing, conditioned by interpretive filters, to the direct connection of fresh seeing. This fresh seeing has a feeling quality; it feels fresh, free, buoyant, and joyful. It feels good. When we open to seeing, we make equivalent images that embody the directness of this perception. But the key point of Nalanda Miksang is the purification of the perceiver and the perceived. This is our contemplative path.

The *inner teachings* of Nalanda Miksang move beyond fresh seeing and experience. With them, we enter the realm of insight. Through practice, experience becomes one with view. We merge our own personal wisdom with the wisdom of the world. Our personal transformation begins to matter. The point of the practice is not so much to feel good as to connect with basic goodness.

We realize that experiences, good or bad, come and go. But insight into things as they are—basic goodness—is vast, profound, and sustaining.

We realize that there is no ultimate special image. Each brilliant image is a multitude. We make thousands of strong and beautiful images, but the ultimate goal of the practice and the Way isn't to make great images.

We realize that continually grasping—for more fresh seeing, good experiences, and brilliant images—itself becomes an obstacle. It gets in the way of subtle and deep transformation.

We realize that fresh seeing, good experiences, and brilliant images can become means for a deeper transformation, not just ends in themselves. Paradoxically, fresh perception, good experience, and brilliant images become even more important, when they aren't about a goal. They are empowered ways to the Way, but they are not the Way itself. Only the Way is the Way.

So the path of transformation builds and moves with a forward vision. The inner teachings transform the outer teachings as a path of empowerment, even as the outer teachings make the inner teaching empowerment possible.

We can say little concerning the secret teachings. They are secret, but we can give some hints. The secret teachings are not hidden or esoteric—they are an open secret.

Everyone always already knows the secret in her own way. *In her own way* is the big hint: Nalanda Miksang will become Nalanda Miksang when you become *you*.

Peace: Synchronization and Harmony

Many people come to dharma, meditation, and contemplative and/or spiritual teachings with the hope of finding peace. This is a good motivation. But what is peace? A tranquil state of mind? Some version of the absence of strife, whether psychological, social, or political? These are common preconceptions about peace. And they are good motivations but compose an inadequate view. What makes us aware of the realization of peace?

The skillful means of the contemplative arts *start* with peace. Nalanda Miksang starts with peace. The whole practice and realization *is* peace.

Here, peace is being connected in communion. It is an ongoing process, an understanding that our wisdom is connected with the wisdom of the world, that our situation is fundamentally good and workable. It is not some sense of union or oneness, but more of a sustained and precise going with the flow. It is the practice of relaxation and sense of humor.

Chögyam Trungpa often speaks of synchronization. In synchronization, we do not lose or dissolve ourselves in wholeness. Rather, we synchronize ourselves with the way things are. We sense how it all fits and where we fit in with how it all fits.

In fact, finding where you fit is finding how it all fits. This is the way of the contemplative arts and Nalanda Miksang. It is simple: when you are color as color, you are you as you. You are there with the *there*. It all fits. The experience of synchronization is balance and peace.

This is personal. It is real experience. It is belonging. Belonging is always just so, intimate and personal. In formal terms, it is the unconditioned within the conditioned. It is simply: Yes.

Instead of the word *peace*, in Nalanda Miksang, we prefer *harmony*. Though we also mean by this a sense of synchronization, *synchronization* can sound slightly mechanical, like synchronizing gears. And *peace* can sound spaced out. *Harmony* is mainly used in music; many sounds can manifest as one sound. Here, being at peace is being in harmony and what we have referred to as being synchronized. Rather than discordant, you find yourself at ease. You connect with the one while retaining the many; your wisdom is in tune with the wisdom of the way things are.

Now-ness is when eye, mind, and phenomenal world are in the same place at the same time. It is not a matter of clock time. This is time suspended within time. It is an unfathomable sense, just being. At that moment, there is just that color, just so, just now. At that moment, you *are* at that moment. It feels good.

Our view is that peace is our fundamental condition. Practice helps us realize that peace. Trying hard to relax does not work. For starters, when you are struggling to find peace, it is the practice of struggle, not the practice of peace. Still, let's start where we are, with our lives and all their challenges. Now, challenges become ways to the Way, not only a way in, but also openings. Often, the very openings we seek are the greatest challenges. They are a walk on the wild side. Opening outside your frame of reference and your comfort zone, they require trust and a sense of adventure.

At peace, you glimpse what it is like to free-fall and simultaneously feel utterly harmonized. Harmonized free fall is an accurate, paradoxical description of deep contemplative practice.

Usually, though, in our day-to-day life, we find that we are partially synchronized and partially distracted. Mind and body are synchronized enough to get us through our life in practical ways, enough to get us through an average day in our average lives.

At the same time, we are distracted. Zen calls this *monkey mind*. Our thoughts and interests flit from one to another. We zoom between current activities, past memories, and future projects. Or our mind simply feels overwhelmed: by passion, depression, anxiety, excitement, and so forth. Captured by our hopes and fears, bored and spaced-out, or bored and seeking entertainment and distraction, we are definitely not at peace.

Usually mind and body operate on autopilot, defaulting to our disconnected, habitual patterns. Think of driving a car—absorbed in thoughts about this or that, somehow you still manage to drive at incredible speeds.

Most of us, most of the time, live the best we can. There is something deeply courageous and poignant about this. It is the salvation of humanity. Yet we are always participating in something beyond our current and ongoing circumstances, something that sustains our very daily circumstances. It's the gift of life—for this particular practice, the gift of vision.

This is not philosophical. It is practical and effective. We have our day in, day out concerns and occupations. These are necessary and good, but we can break through, take a real break from these patterns.

Of course, if you are an air traffic controller, it is probably best that at work you focus on the screen rather than on the play of light on the wall! However, most of us are not on the job all the time, even when we are on the job; most of us treat life as the "job" of living. Yet what about the everyday magical possibilities we could allow ourselves? They are ongoing. The possibilities of possibilities are an everyday adventure.

Our life is not average. It is unique and sacred and worth fully appreciating. Deep down we know this. Contemplative photography is a way to connect with our contemplative mind, the mind that *knows this*—the heart that *knows this*.

LIGHT, TEXTURE, and PATTERN ASSIGNMENTS

ASSIGNMENT TWO: THE WAY OF LIGHT

We are moving on to another key feature of the visual world: light.

The word *photography* means, "inscribing with light." We see because of light. The eye developed as an organ that senses and works with light and space. Without light, we are in the dark. Some also call photography the art of light and shadow. Many of the skills in photography are techniques of managing light.

For contemplative photography, light is a major subject. We can use it to notice light through the day and the seasons. Light expresses tremendous ordinary magic. It highlights space and form; it invites tone and moods.

Some teachings in Nalanda Miksang were only hinted at in the Color as Color assignment. The light assignments explore these more deeply. In particular, the light assignments bridge levels one and two, rather than using level one only.

The heart of Nalanda Miksang manifests more at level two, and the light assignment opens the main practice of this path: the exploration of the phenomenal world in level two.

Starting with level one, first you will explore light abstractly, as a form. Then you will move to the expressive engagement of level two light.

PART ONE—LIGHT AS LIGHT: PATCHES OF LIGHT AND SHADOW

In general, approach this assignment in the same way as you did with color: start with view, motivation and intent. Then, engage the practices of synchronization, looking and seeing, and flash of perception.

Our first practice is just noticing light and working with light as light.

Light is miraculously pervasive. It literally lights up and opens our visual world. The eye opens to light and space. Even color is a modulation of light.

So we have to find a way to keep light simple. Your first assignment: photograph patches of light or patches of shadow, for instance, a patch of light on a wall, created when light comes through a window or a pattern of shadow created by leaves. Very simple. Very ordinary.

Patch of light is a phrase. The shape does not have be a single patch of light. It can be stripes or bars of light, dots of light, and so forth. The point is: keep it simple. Start with the level one orientation of just contacting the visual as visual: light as light—noticing light, looking at light, and seeing light.

At this point, forget aesthetics. Don't try to make beautiful images. Just engage the discipline of seeing light as light.

Seeing and photographing light as light shows us the aesthetics and many moods of light very naturally. This illuminates our images, making them beautiful. First, become intimate with light. Then, you can enter the spell of light's enchantment.

Noticing a simple patch of light gives you a focus. This simplifies the quandary of how to work with light when it is everywhere, all the time. You are less likely to look for the aesthetic effects of light and more likely to strengthen your discrimination of light as light. Rather than mixing light with color or other forms, you're more able to see light as light, engaging your contemplative intention.

Try to do this assignment in the early or late part of the day. The sun's lower angle is more conducive to patch of light. As light streams through openings in walls and buildings, it shows the world of light and shadows. The same holds true if you are shooting indoors. At the edges of the day, you may notice more patches of light inside.

Sometimes the patch of light will also be a patch of color. That's fine. In part, this is why we work with color first. Realize that it is the patch of light that makes the patch of color. Without the light, we would not see the color. Rarely do we get a single form of perception—color, light, or texture—by itself. Simply see what comes first and what your main perception is. The review process will aid in this synchronization.

Color also comes first in assignments because, in terms of craft and technique, light is more demanding. This simple approach to light gives everyone a way in.

If you feel comfortable in your camera craft, you can go ahead with the assignment. Take the same contemplative approach as you did with color. Remember to fill the frame with the flash of perception, your perception of a patch of light or a patch of shadow. We strongly suggest you turn off your camera's flash. The flash on a camera is there to even out differences between light and dark. It will change the image, so it won't match your perception.[2]

On the level of perception, another question can arise: Am I perceiving light or shadow? A Patch of light always includes a context of shadow, and vice versa. Imagine a latticework of squares of light, with bars of shadow. Is the perception of patches of light? Or bars of shadow?

Light and shadow always manifest together. This is basically a background/foreground issue—whether we see a patch of light or a patch of shadow depends on the focus of the perception. If the shadow serves as background, then we see the photo as a patch of light and vice versa: if the light serves as background, it shows a patch of shadow. Light or shadow? This is part of the training in visual discrimination. Sometimes light and shadow are evenly matched, as in a grid pattern of light squares. Then either perception is possible.

Don't forget: where you stand when you catch a flash of perception and where you stand to frame its equivalent can be very far apart. One scenario is that you catch a flash of perception, a large patch of light on a wall far across the parking lot. If you shoot it from where you were when the flash occurred, the picture would be of the wall surrounded by other things. So, move closer. Fill your frame with the patch of light.

---

2 Please see our appendix for suggestions on contemplative camera craft.

As with color, intend to notice light even when you are not doing the assignment. Notice light in an ordinary way. Forget like or dislike, forget aesthetics and camera craft. Maybe don't even photograph it. Simply notice light as an ordinary phenomenal form, as an appearance, the way it comes and goes. What difference does noticing light make in your day-to-day life? Are you aware of the light? Does light spark your awareness?

Start to notice light as light. This discernment becomes more evident in the image review. Is it a presentation of light or of something else? For example, the image may be a patch of lit-up color surrounded by shadow. But in this case, the patch of light allows the patch of color to manifest. So the patch of light is primary. Purify the eye and clarify the mind in discerning light as light, and conversely, by discerning light as light, purify the eye and clarify the mind.

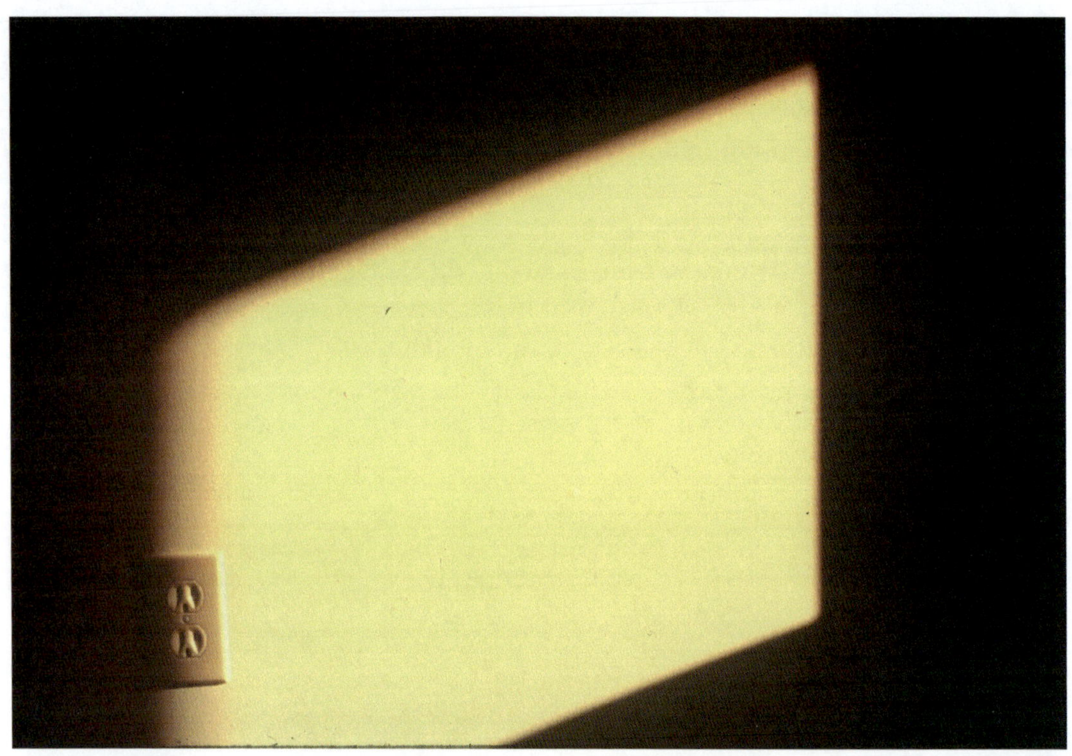

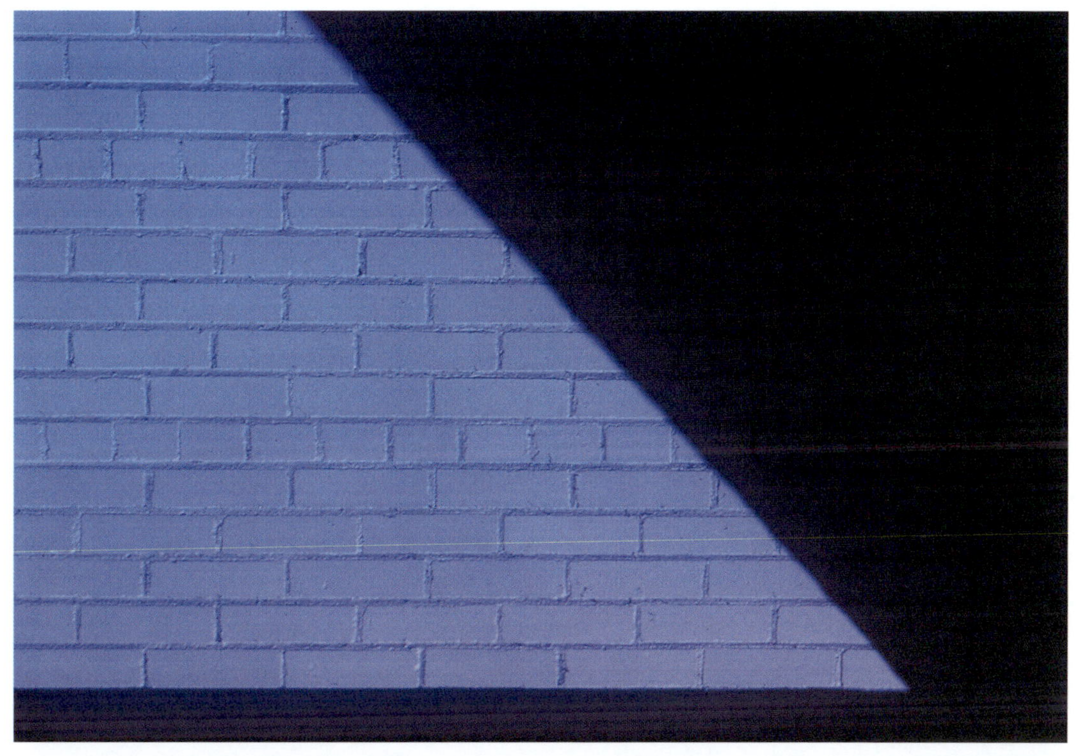

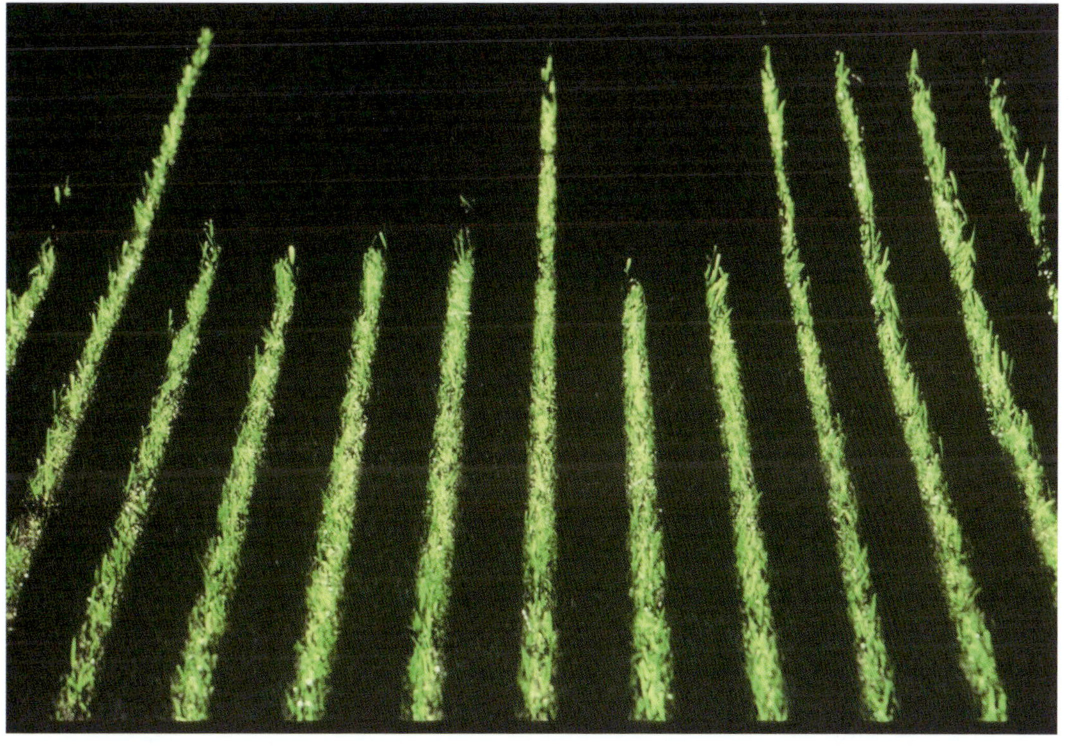

In these example images, we can see a variety of what a simple prompt opens up. Patches of light can slowly reveal the "ordinary world" to us, like in the first photo, while still being about the light. Patches of shadow can reveal a lot about the object they are the shadow of, but again, remaining mostly about the shadow, as in the second photo. In the third photo, we see that patches of light and shadow often appear with color, and finally, in four, we can see a pattern of alternating light and shadow.

PERSONAL STORY: MIRIAM

In weekend programs, we send students home to do the light assignment in the evenings and mornings. When I was teaching a level one course in Philadelphia, a student came in on Sunday morning with her Patch of Light/Shadow images and a gleam in her eye. She described going to a local park that she hadn't been to before. She saw a young man popping his skateboard over what she thought were curbs or bumps in the sidewalk. She saw regular intervals of dark and light. Perhaps they had set up some kind of obstacle course for skaters?

What was going on in the conceptual world sense was that tall trees lined the walk the skateboarder was on. These trees cast long, dark, and solid shadows in regular intervals across the sidewalk. The skater knew this, of course. He was playing with his own perception as well as hers. He used the shadows as opportunities to practice jumping on his board.

She didn't get a photograph, but it didn't matter. The experience touched her deeply. It did all of us, creating such a bold image in our minds as good as if we had been there. And more than an image, she "showed" us the understanding, the deep knowing that is almost indescribable, delivered with playfulness from the phenomenal world that things are not as they seem. That can be very good news.

PART TWO—OPENING UP LIGHT: FORMS AND THE MAGIC OF LIGHT

We introduced you to the study of light in the last assignment. Specifically, discerning light as light and crafting an image of that.

The next exercise is another light assignment, a further exploration of light. Let's build on our first light assignment by taking it in another direction.

The whole week, as you were noticing light, perhaps you began to develop a feeling for light in all its many shades and appearances—the fresh, clean feel of the light on crystal clear mornings; the soft light on misty mornings; the sometimes-buttery quality of light; the moods of light—the warm mood or mysterious mood—and the many colors and shades of late daylight; the play of light and shadows throughout the day, such as the brightness of the midday sun; how magically a splash of light can transform a room, bring out its already-existing magic; how the play of light illuminates a street scene; and so on. There are endless displays of light.

In this second light assignment, we move from a simpler study to a contemplation of light. Contemplation involves reflection, appreciation, and insight, not just of light, but also of perception. Begin to consider that the source of contemplation is perception itself—perception, which is neither here or there. Instead, it is contact and connection. We can speak of moods of light and so forth, but now we can start to see how light also opens the world of sensibility.

Let's investigate light in a more deliberate way. Light delivers the visual world as the visual world, the just that/just so phenomenal world. Light works with form, illuminating the things and surfaces of the world, which makes things visible to us, but also connects us to the mood of that moment, that light, and that object.

This teaching is part of a more general contemplative teaching on things. In particular, we become interested in the manifestation of things as visual phenomena. What does that mean? If we pay attention, we see that things never remain the same. Perception shows us how things continually change, manifesting in different ways. This is already fresh and free. Seeing this is already contemplative.

By contemplating the fluid way of light and form we step into the rays of the free-flowing phenomenal world.

And we can go a step further. We can see the phenomenal world as the phenomenal world, free of reference to things. See the phenomenal world as it is: expressive and fluid. These expressions have a natural aesthetic, and we are naturally liberated when we open to it. This points us to a Way: a Way for contemplative art and the contemplative artist. It is not a special Way. It is a natural Way. The Way of the phenomenal world is always already available to everyone. The light assignment helps us enter and deepen our connection to it.

Now let's shift from patches of light and shadow to the play of light and form. Sometimes a form is literally highlighted (a vase, a door, a dog) so it catches your eye. Sometimes the light itself is striking; then, your attention includes the form. This play of light and form invites a response. This noticing and responding to the quality of the light or the presence of the form illuminates some aspect of mind and the phenomenal world. For instance, in the sunlight, John notices the red highlights in his Chinese daughter's dark hair. He sees that she is also Irish.

So the assignment is to notice and explore the effect of front light, sidelight, and backlight in relation to form. We follow a traditional photography presentation in Nalanda Miksang. The key to the relationship with light on form is the direction: front, side, and back. However, each direction also opens an understanding of our world in a different way. Light and form work together to present the phenomenal world. In part, this is how the phenomenal world always appears to us. It is a blend of elements. It is not a thing; it is the now effect of a just that/just so blend of constantly changing factors.

Included in the assignment is the camera craft of working with these different forms of light.[3]

Front light

Front light is light that shines on something in front of you. From your perspective, it is coming from behind you. It illuminates the surface you face. Sometimes it is called *direct light*. Usually front light is bold, a strong light that makes forms seem more solid. Actually, this is the front light making it seem flat and even. Or the effect can be pacifying, subtler. This is usually due to a pervasive flood of evenly distributed light, which is directly reflected back at you. Perceptually, though, it's as if the light dissolves into the form.

Overall, direct light diminishes the presence of shadow area and the range of tones, which, in turn, perceptually diminishes the sense of contrast. Without contrast, the presentation of form is perceptually flattened, either solidly or softly.

Which of these effects manifests will often depend on the context. For instance, if the form is isolated and has a lighter tone than the background (for instance, a light yellow brick chimney in a deep blue sky), then the light will tend to monumentalize (solidify) the form. If it is a large field of grasses, the field may actually feel softer thanks to the overall front light.

The classic photographer Ansel Adams used this quality of light often and to dramatic effect. Look at his photograph of the Mormon Temple, the stark-white façade of the building against the dark sky. A form that was already a monument to the glory of God is further monumentalized. Edward Weston also worked with this kind of light. The subdued contrast created by strong front light makes forms appear more like space.

For this contemplative exercise, don't to worry about effect. Simply tune in to this quality: strong front light can monumentalize form. Notice also that strong front light, as in the second example image, can seem to flatten form altogether.

Conventional photographers often avoid front light. It provides little drama. But this flat aesthetic has a unique equilibrium for the contemplative photographer. We will explore it further in level three and Absolute Eye.

Technique and craft for front light is straightforward. Generally, you want to expose for the light. This highlights the form, showing us form as an image, whether monumental or spacious.

---

3 Please see our appendix for suggestions on contemplative camera craft.

This light on form assignment often inspires images that feel more level two. Light on form reveals an aspect of *things in the world*. Still, focus on perception as much as possible. Remember, you are not documenting a lit-up something. You are tuning in to its phenomenal expression.

As we can see in the two example images of front light, front light perceptually flattens surfaces. In the first image we see how the building appears even more solid, monumentalized by the front light. The second image contains a chimney that we know has depth, but the front light has erased that depth. Perceptually, the chimney appears pasted on.

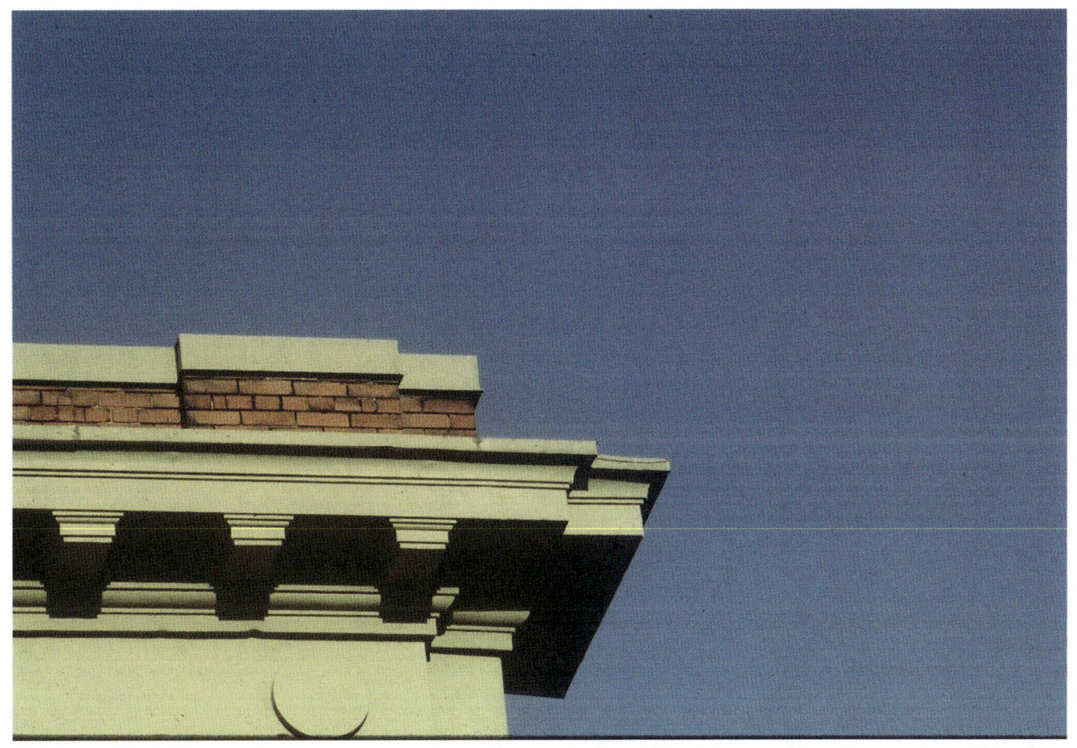

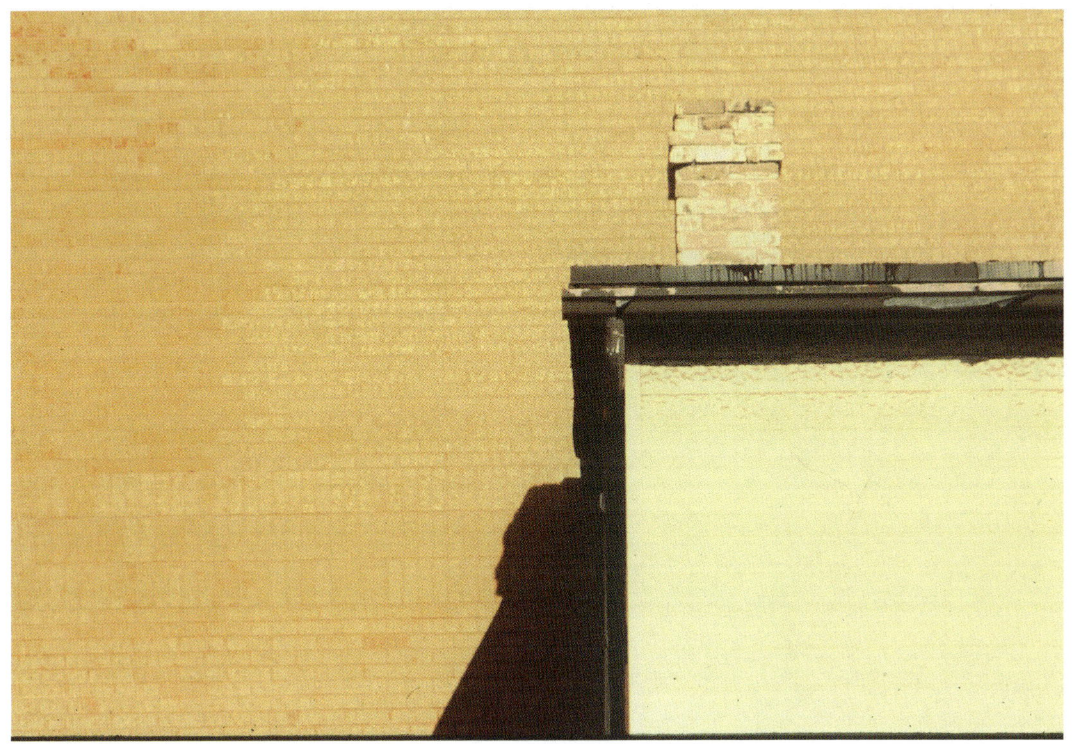

Sidelight

Sidelight highlights contour and shows us shape. This light plays with form. Creating either strong or gradual contrasts in tone, it highlights the drama of light and shadow. Sidelight catches an edge and spills over the rest of the surface. Sidelight caresses a form, so it emerges as a shape with volume. If a form is textured—what in front light appears as a flat surface—it is transformed in sidelight into a tapestry of light and shadow. The long lines of shadow that sometimes come with sidelight are themselves intriguing. They can compliment or distort the form.

A splash or caress of sidelight transforms the feeling tone of a form or the ambience of a scene. This light expresses mood and magic. It articulates the inner glow of a visual presence. It translates the sensuality and shape of a subject, whether landscape, interior of a house, or a person's face. This is why much of the craft in professional photography and dramatic arts replicates the transformative power of this lighting. Sidelight brings out the elegance of a still life in paintings of the Dutch masters. Sidelight is how we see the shapes of dancers on a stage. This is also the preferred lighting for portrait photographers, bringing out the character of the face.

The contemplative photographer simply appreciates the natural magic of this light, which invites the eye and heart to the endless drama of light, shadow, and form.

Exposure for sidelight is subtler than for front light. You are working with the play of light and shadow. In front lighting, you learned how to expose for light. Now you have to include shadow if that's what your perception is. As always, focus on making a duplicate of the perception. Was it light, or was it shadow?[4] If seeing the shadow area was a part of your flash of perception, then expose for that. Open your exposure, let in more light, to make visible whatever is in the shadow area. This isn't like Patch of Light, where you went with strong contrast. Here, be subtler. Wasn't the perception subtler?

Come back to the flash of perception. What did you see? Was it direct and bold, a stark contrast of light and shadow? Or did you see a more delicate, subtle tone and texture?

Recognize the flash of perception and work from there. If the perception is strong light and strong shadow, then expose for the light just as instructed. If the perception is dramatic—the contrast of light and shadow—then make a dramatic image.

Much more than front light, sidelight begins to reveal the world of level two, with its heartfelt perceptions, but more about this in a moment.

You can see here how sidelight truly brings out shape and form. In fact, form used to be a separate assignment in level one, but we found that what brings out form is, in fact, sidelight. You can see how sidelight is a key part of texture. Without the sidelight, we would not see the separate parts of the siding. Seeing texture is, in fact, seeing light and shadow on a more intimate scale.

---

4 Please see our appendix for suggestions on contemplative camera craft.

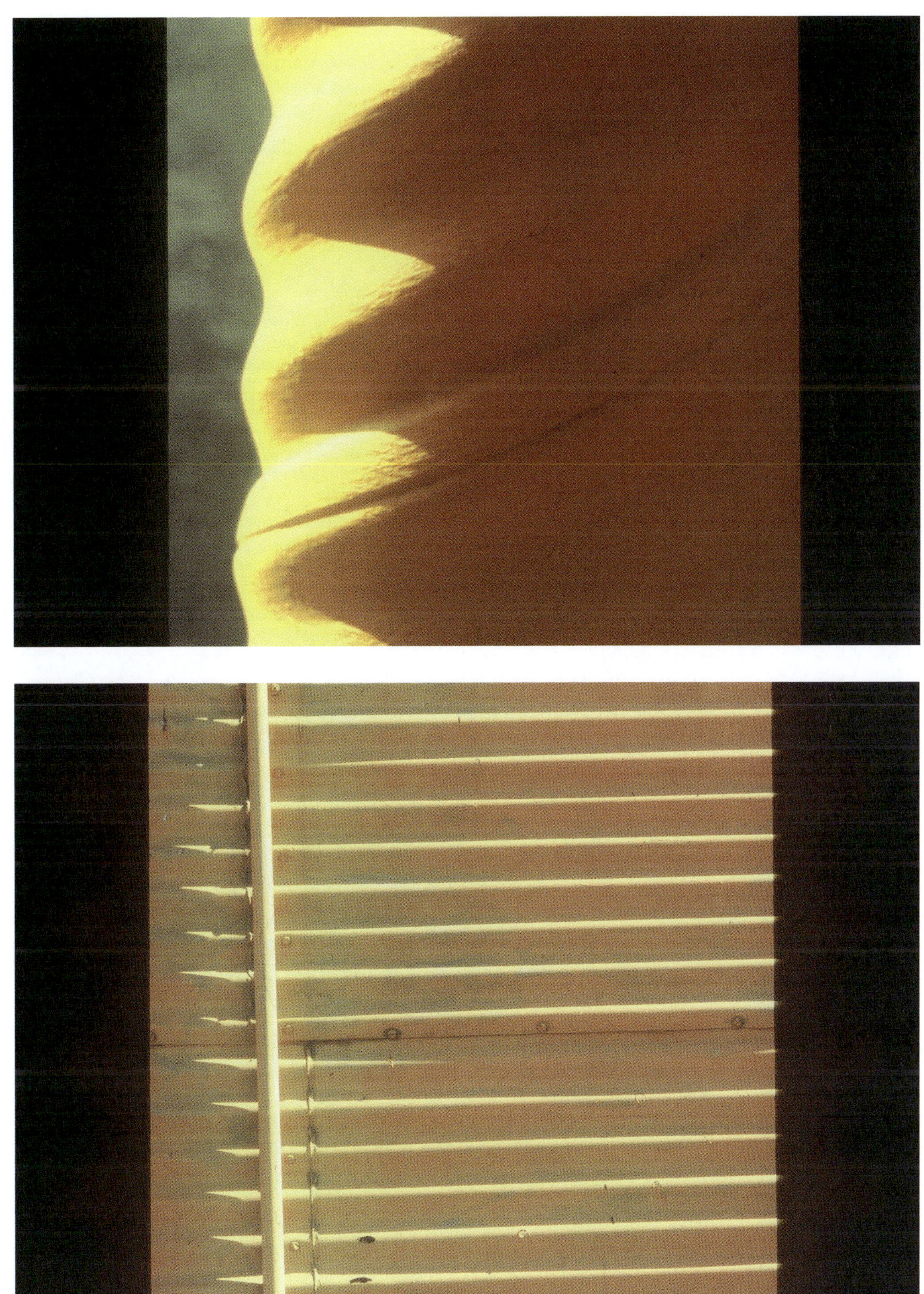

Backlight

If sidelight is drama, then backlight is opera. It is dramatic to the extreme; it can make a form appear light and airy or definite and bold, and sometimes both at the same time. Backlighting illuminates translucent forms and silhouettes solid forms.

Nature presents the magic of backlight every day. Backlighting makes a simple strand of grass come alive. Picture this: light silhouetting a closed purple tulip (because it is opaque), shining through each drop of water that clings to its petals after a spring shower. Backlit, the broken pod of milkweed seems both solid in the center and ethereal around the edges. A large bed of tulips manifests as stained glass. Even a backyard filled with white dandelions reveals its magic, if we drop our weeding agenda and simply look.

Look up into a tall maple tree, where leaves hang at different angles. When thinner leaves are backlit, the green and other colors pop as light illuminates them, making them glow. Wherever the leaves overlap, the shapes become solid forms and are impenetrable to light. Here, also, the effects of front light, sidelight, and backlight combine. Front light includes the reflection of direct light that falls on the leaves. Those leaves glisten and shine, green and solid, while backlit leaves glow a softer green or become black where they overlap. More than just maple leaves, you see a kaleidoscope of light expressing reality.

Not only nature has this magic. Many urban forms are transformed by backlight—laundry on the line, sunlight entering a room through windows and catching on the curtains, light seeping through flags and banners, awnings and umbrellas. And then there is the most dramatic of urban backlit arts: stained glass. Dramatically or subtly, stained glass invites in the glow of backlighting to make the sacred spaces of cathedrals glow. In winter, nature's own spontaneous stained glass occurs as frost on backlit windows.

It always begins with perception. What is the phenomenal world displaying? What do you see? Once you have figured out your flash of perception, make your light settings match the light striking the object from behind.[5]

Backlight is the most difficult lighting to capture in terms of craft. But capturing it accurately makes for very rewarding images in the long run. More importantly, it connects us to a magic that literally seems to hide behind the thing world that surrounds us all the time. The magic isn't actually the backlight – but what it reveals to us.

The first image shows us the opera of milkweed lit from behind. The second shows us how backlight can bring out the intensity of color and radiance through fabric

---

5   Please see our appendix for suggestions on contemplative camera craft.

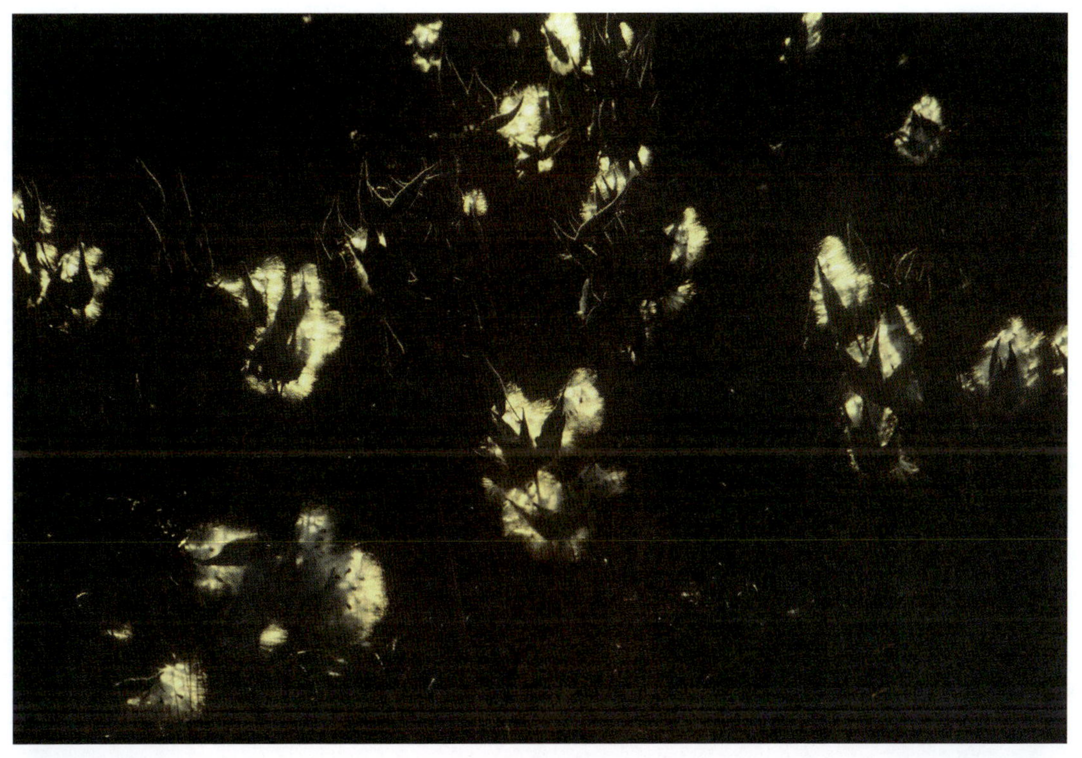

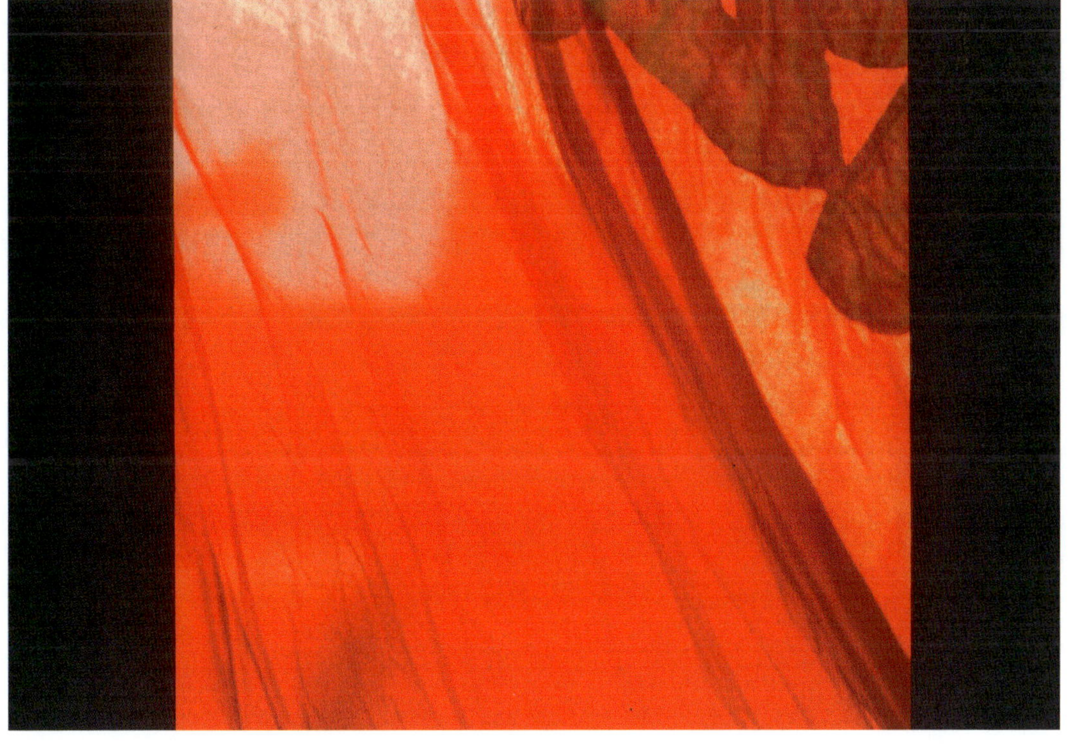

PART THREE—OPENING UP LIGHT: LEVEL TWO

The basic assignment for light on form in Nalanda Miksang is already quite large: front light, sidelight, and backlight. The effect of light on form is a subtler subject, so we usually allow two weeks for this exploration.

Whether you do Patch of Light or Front Light, Sidelight, or Backlight first is up to you. Explore each in its own session or many of them in one session. Regardless, enjoy becoming familiar with all of light's appearances, and see how they transform your sense of the world.

Contemplating the way of light dramatically demonstrates the difference between the conceptual world of things and the phenomenal world. Focusing on form opens up the range of what you see and also the depth of your appreciation. This is the second level of perception, and level two of Nalanda Miksang.

A stucco wall lit by sidelight looks like a stucco wall; you can see its roughness. That same wall lit with front light looks flat, not like stucco. So here is the contemplative question: Which is the real wall? Experience tells us there is no such thing as the same wall. The phenomenal forms of the world, in this case a stucco wall, are ever changing.

It is the same concerning how light works with color. Objectively, the yellow wall on the opposite page is all the same color, but which is the real yellow? Is it the lemon yellow? There is no objective color. Reality is a world of experience and participation. Color isn't really objective, and yet neither is this seeing subjective. Seeing is a fluid and lively exchange between experience and the phenomenal world.

The Way of light assignments also open up space of light, how light happens in the context of space. In a level two way, light is often highlighting a scene rather than the subject matter itself. It makes the situation interesting without necessarily being the focus of attention. The drama of light transforms the sensibility of a setting. It changes the space completely. The world of things is a phenomenal world of circumstances. A world full of magic—as it always was.

Most of the following level two light images would fit into the category or assignment we call "Ordinary Personal World." Much of level two is exploring the phenomenal world with our fresh and free eyes, developed in level one. So you can see here that the subjects of these photographs are objects—a cat toy, a flower, and so on—but not really. Actually, the subjects are the play of light with the phenomena. Perceptions are always the actual subject in any Nalanda Miksang photograph.

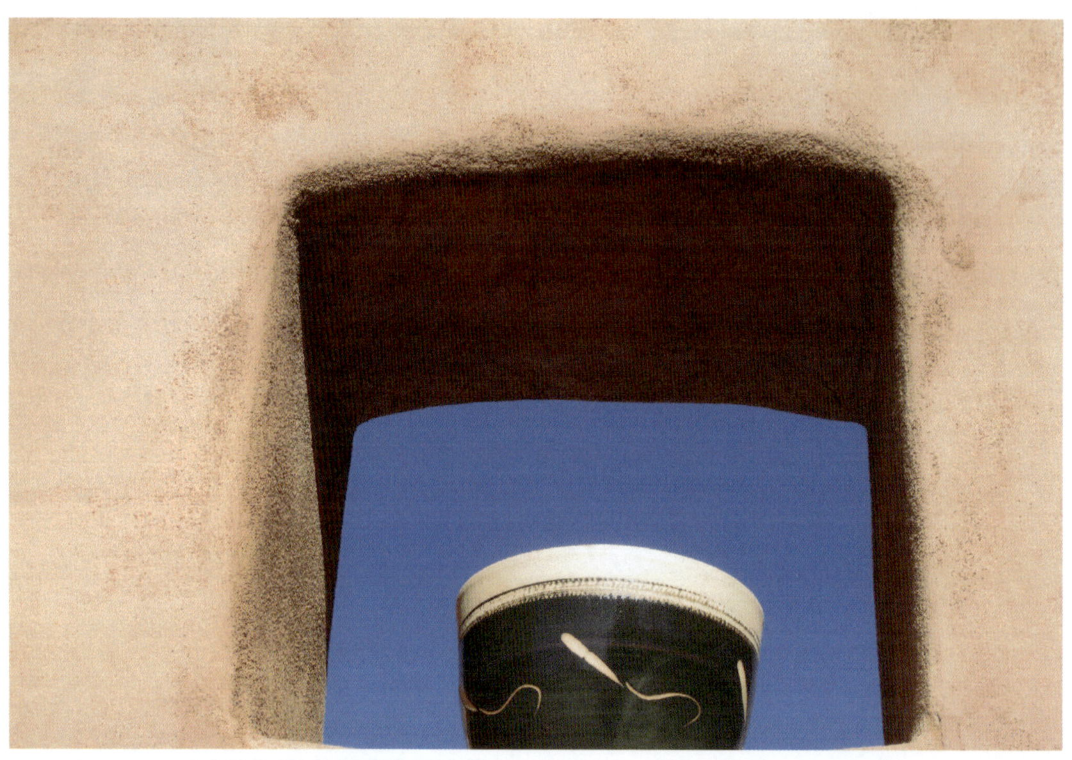

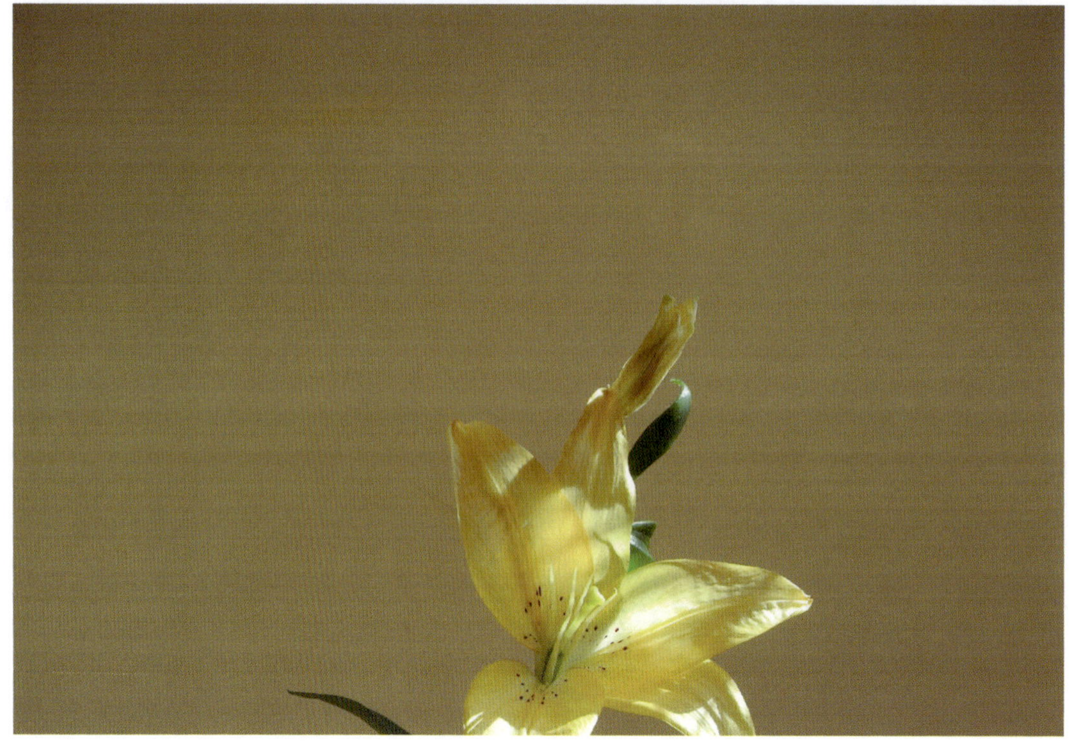

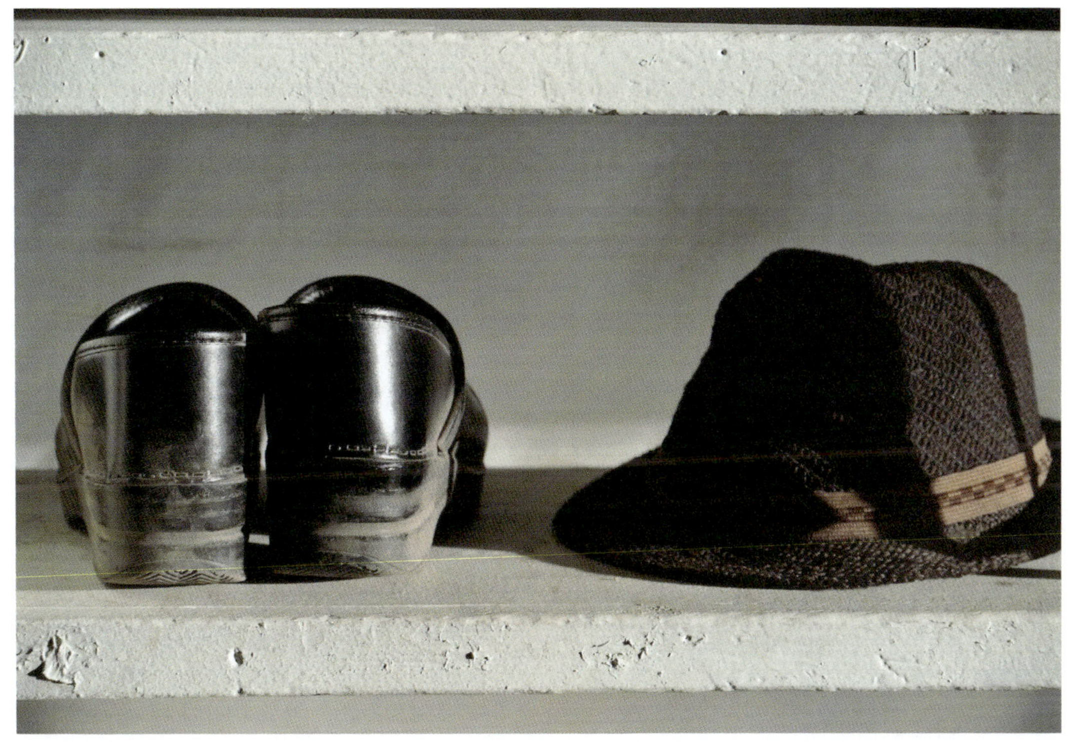

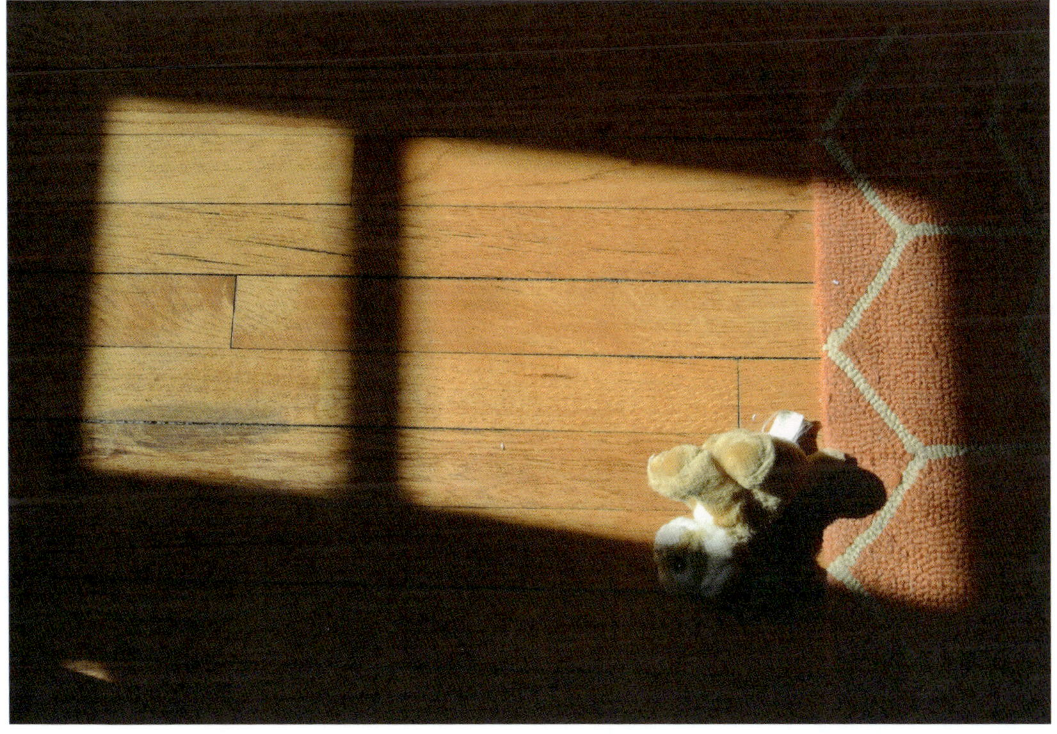

PERSONAL STORY: MIRIAM

The other day, I woke up a few minutes before my alarm. The sun was just beginning to rise. The early dawn light was blue and cool, and it was bright enough to welcome me. Then I saw the first lick of yellow/orange/gold on a tree across the street.

Unable to believe that this was what it appeared to be—the sun—I kept watching. As the sun rose, the liquid richness dripped down the trunk of a tree. I couldn't believe it. Was that the sun? Yes. Then other trees slid into the scene, first in front of this one, then behind, until both those across the street and those right in front of our window were all lit from a sideways/back angle that made their right sides shine as though gilded. Transfixed, I waited to see what would light up next.

And then it hit me.

The sun rises every day. This is ordinary, usual, expected. It is also miraculous, magical, and gorgeous. I swear that in the ten years I have lived in this house, I had never ever seen such beauty in those trees. The dreary late-February drab of broken, bare branches fell away. Yet it was the same world, the same window I look out of every morning—the same sun. And also not. Never the same.

Diffuse Light and Saturated Color

Sometimes light is not directional. In certain weather conditions, especially cloudy weather, it is diffuse, with an even sense of overall-ness. In terms of visual appearance, it lessens contrast and softens the presence of forms.

Front light can also diminish the sense of contrast but with a different effect: flatness. So diffuse light and front light open up different perceptual worlds. The flattening of front light can actually make an object seem more solid. The softness of diffuse light gives a sense of overall evenness to tonal values and, therefore, a sense of spaciousness. Images can result that are gentle, soothing, and mysterious.

Certain kinds of diffuse light enhance the power of color. After a rainstorm, when it is still overcast but the clouds lighten, light seems luminous. Especially when combined with wet surfaces, colors seem vivid, saturated. They seem to be bleeding into the phenomenal world.

What a great circumstance to try for more color exploration!

In these two diffuse light images, we can see how light after a rain can help color pop, and how a softer, diffuse light on a mellow color creates a lot of space.

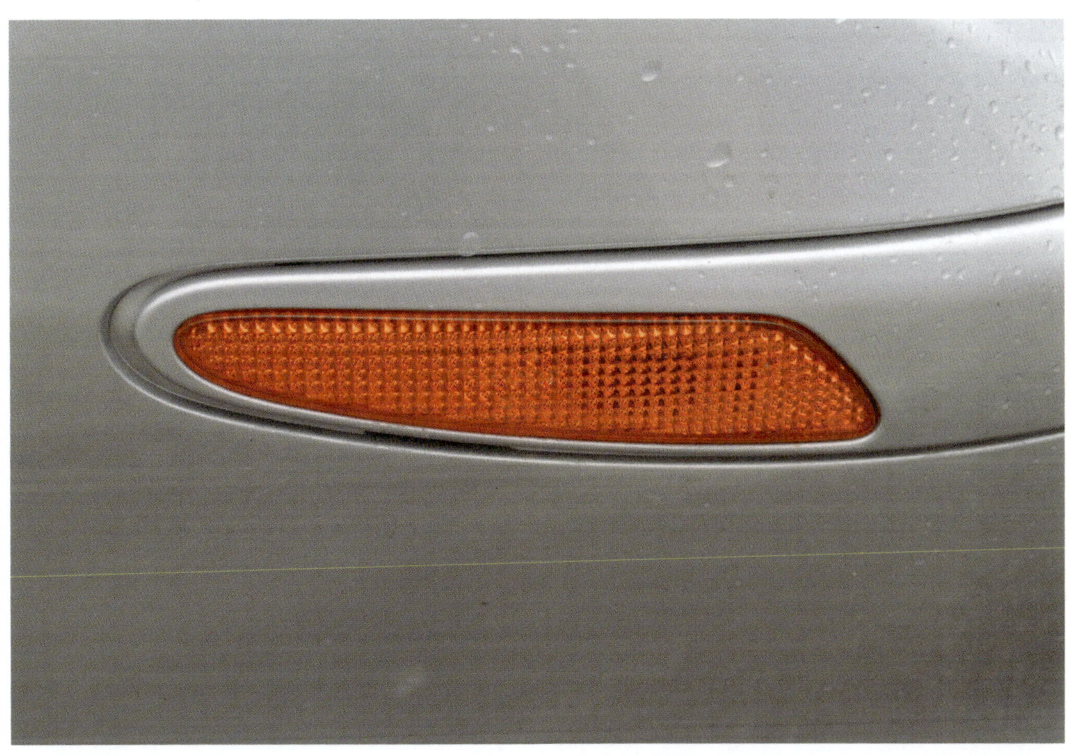

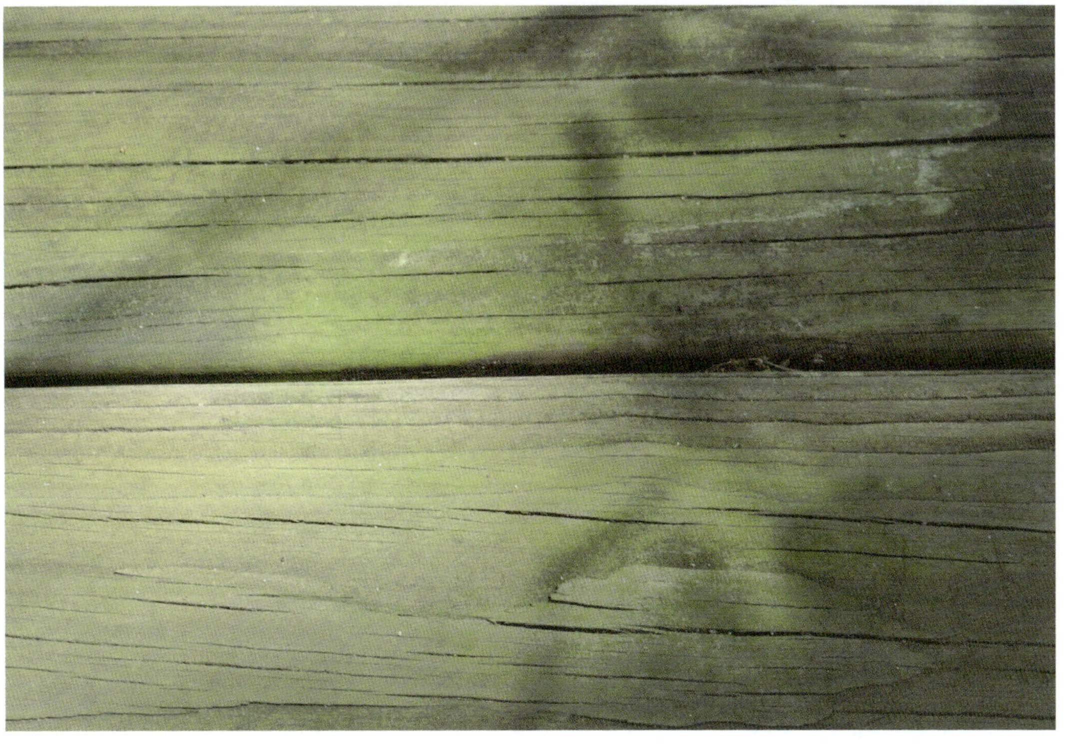

Opening Up Color

Through exploring light, we develop a better sense of our perceptual levels: the simplicity and directness of the literal manifestation in level one, and the full and open expressiveness of level two. For the Color as Color assignment, we held strictly to the level one focus: direct contact and simplicity. Now it's time to revisit color in a more tangible and open way. In Color Plus, we move to level two to explore the forms, contexts, and scenes of the experienced world, all via color. Here, you experience color as the dominant, or major contributing, element. Time to include some of the fire engine or the reflective facets of a red-and-white car taillight or a yellow chimney against a deep blue sky—there are endless enticing possibilities.

Open to the full Way of color and enhance your view of the phenomenal world. The many hues and saturations of color turn the world brilliant and attractive. A kaleidoscope, it attracts the eye and enriches the mind.

Again, the images that further explore level one assignments often fit into what we would call level two. Notice that even though these are images that include a broom, a bucket, and a flower vase, they are actually photographs of the play of color and space, not just documentary pictures of the objects.

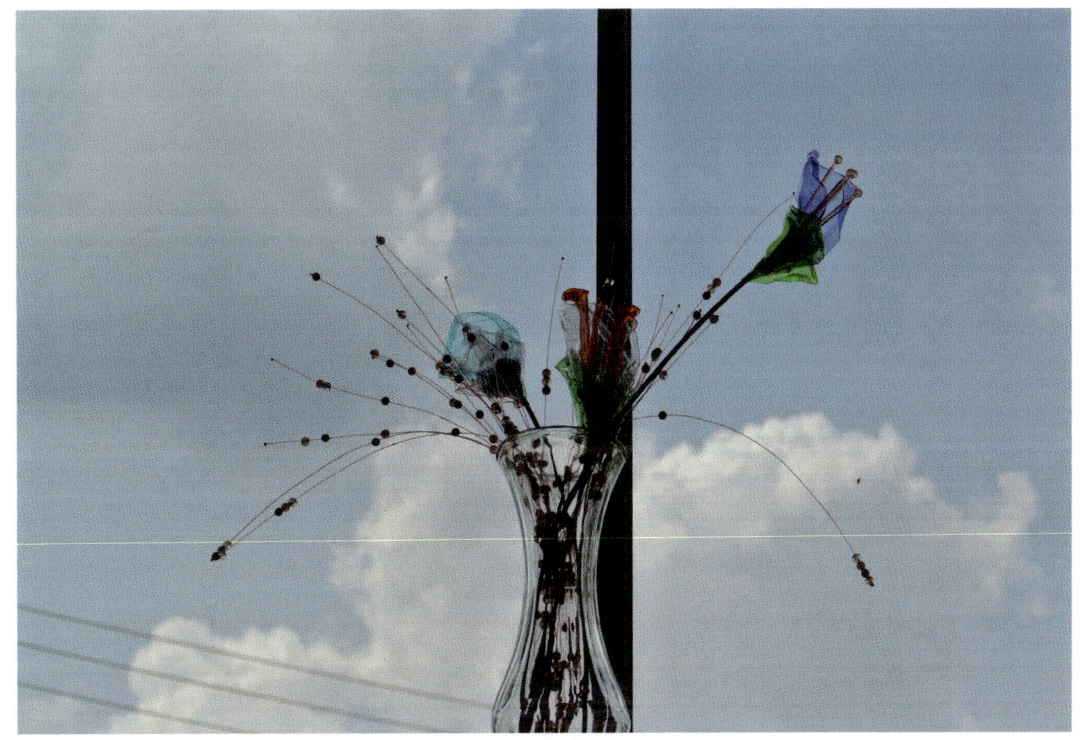

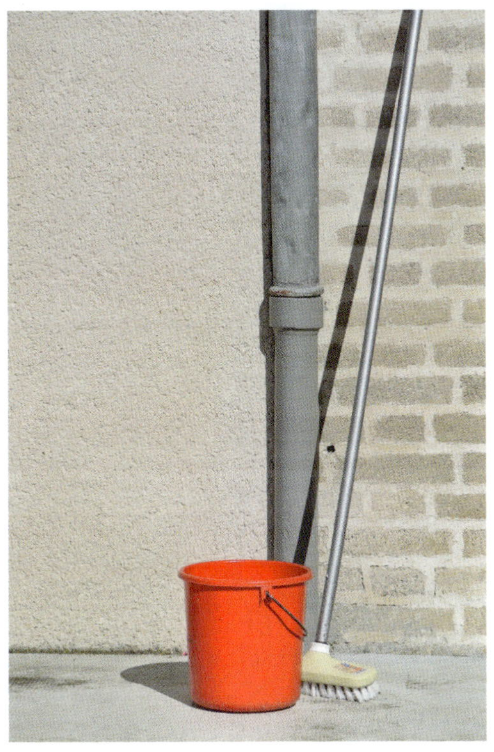

ASSIGNMENT THREE: FORMS OF SURFACE: TEXTURE AND PATTERN

Time to consider the forms of surface. Seeing always includes a surface. Vision arrives and comes to rest on a surface. The specific qualities of surface include texture, pattern, and even shape. In exploring sidelight, we saw some exploration of shape.

Let's investigate texture and pattern.

Visual Texture

You were briefly introduced to texture when we explored light, in particular sidelight. Recall that sidelight highlights the tangible feeling of forms through the contrast of light and shadow. In contrast, in diffuse or front light, a pile of sharp rocks can seem soft.

Now we focus on experiencing and photographing the quality of visual tangibility. In this assignment, we explore the overlap between the world we see and the world we touch.

When observing an image of pure visual/tactile texture, a viewer should feel as if she is touching it with her eyes: rough, smooth, soft, hard, squishy, sticky, sharp, etc. In other words, the image should directly transmit texture to her eyes.

This is not as straightforward as it seems. It's time for a good lesson in the difference between concept and perception, the difference between what you know and what you show. For example, consider a form we know has a tactile quality: a brick wall with a rough surface. We know the surface will feel rough to the touch. We know we can feel the grooves between the bricks.

With sidelight, we see and sense this. But what if the wall is front lit? With front light, in visual terms, it looks flat with a regular pattern. Instead of conveying a strong sense of rough texture, it shows only a flat visual pattern. You know that it is textured. But you do not *see* the texture.

So, here is further training in visual discernment: Do not look for things that you know have texture. Actually look and see the texture.

You must perceive this texture and show this perception in an image. Again, notice that what counts is the perception. In general, texture feels different than, say, color. Color tends to be more definite and dramatic. Remember our slogan: it stops the eye and stops the mind. This is partly why we present it as the first assignment; it's a good starting place for experiencing the flash of perception. With texture, a flash of perception still occurs but usually with a softer landing. When exploring texture, take your time to feel your way with it.

Different textures offer different sensibilities. How does your eye feel when you see a pile of sharp rocks, the dark shadows and bright highlights proclaimed by sidelight? How does the eye react when it encounters that same pile of rocks bathed in diffuse light, looking more like a pile of soft, gray forms?

Never forget: the main point is to see texture and show texture. Feel how texture is a distinctive feature that informs our visual world.

A fundamental teaching of Nalanda Miksang is the difference between the conceptual/objective world we take for granted and the phenomenal world, the moment-by-moment world of experience.

These texture images show a wide range of textures, but all give us a direct visual experience of texture. Our eyes can literally feel what it would feel like to touch the bumpiness, the slickness, the furriness, the metalic-ness.

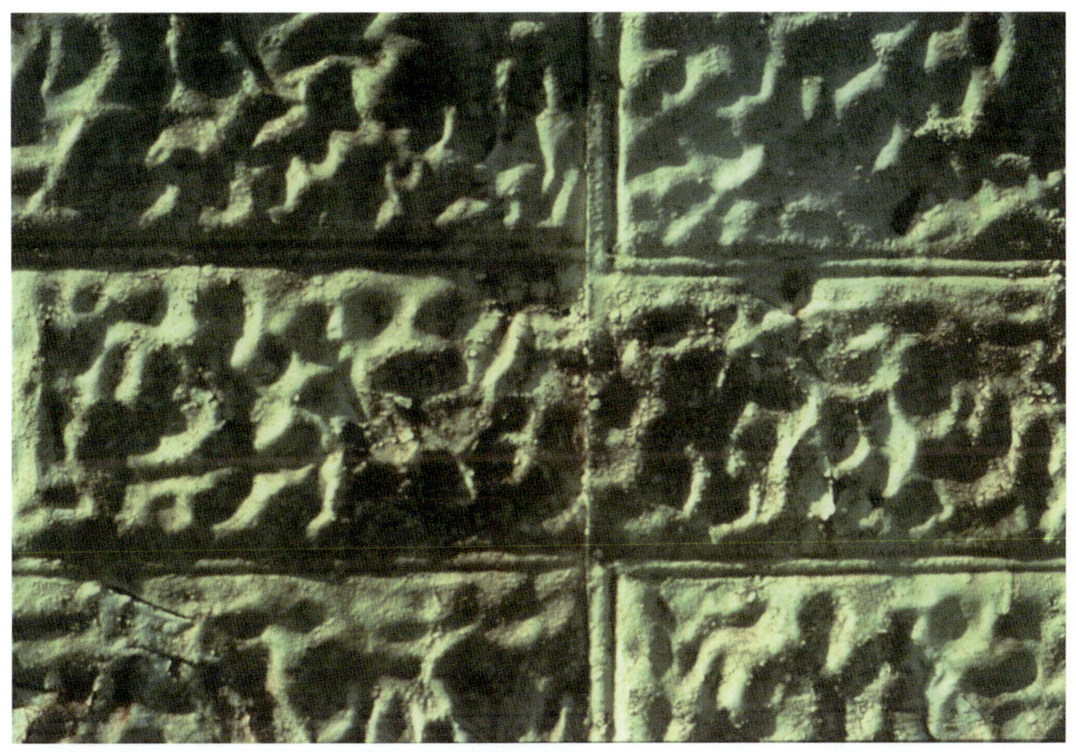

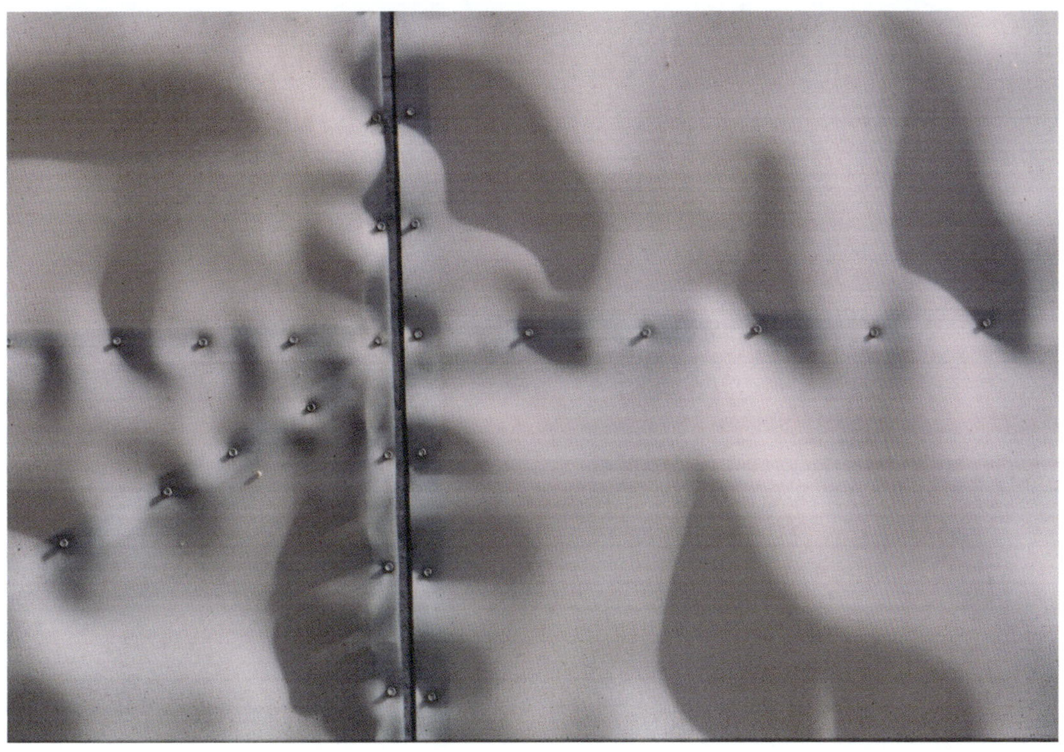

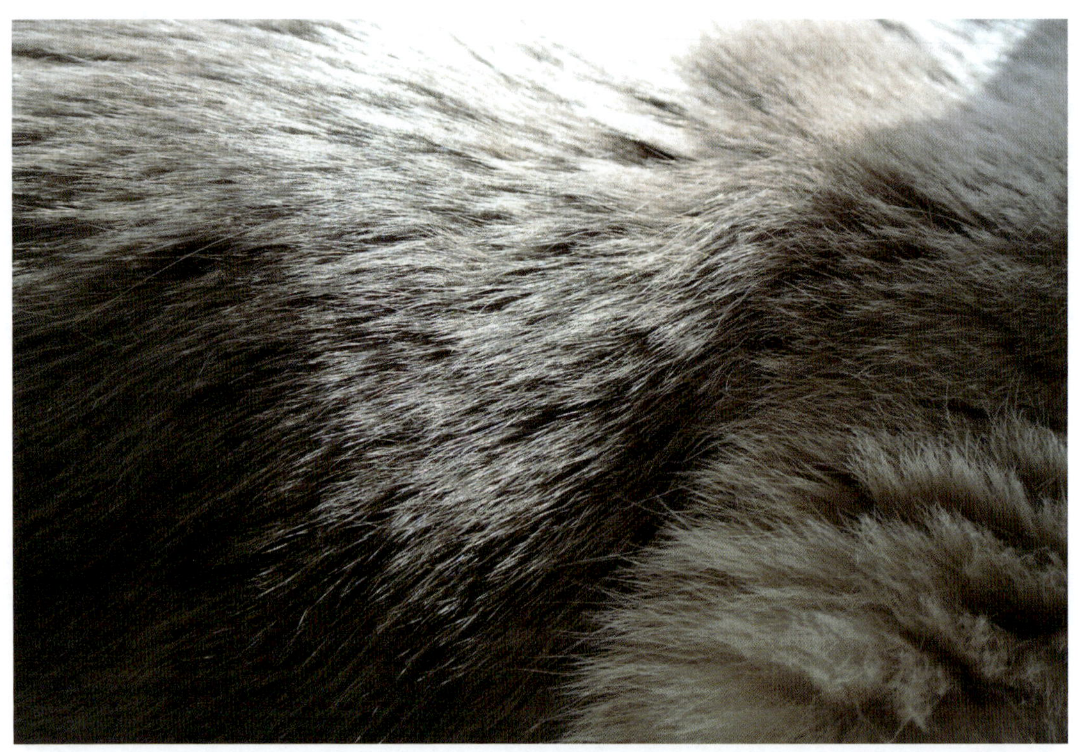

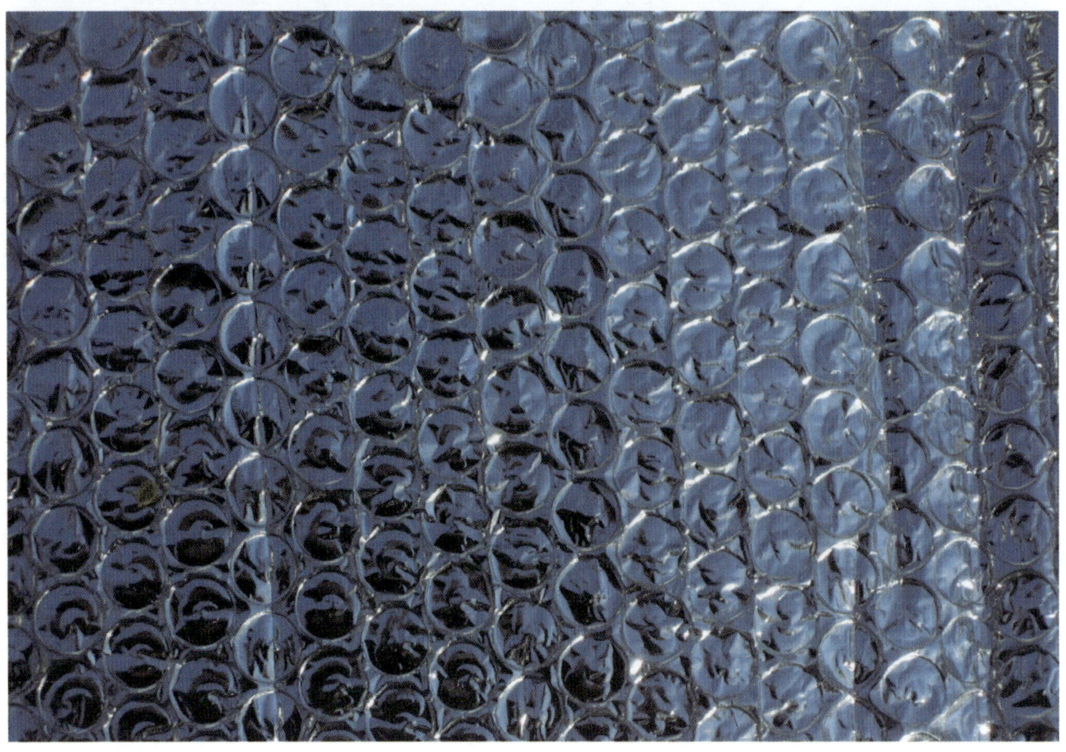

Pattern

Pattern is usually the easiest assignment. It is also fun and creative. So far, you have been working hard to train in the basic elements of the visual world. Now it's time to relax and enjoy playing with pattern.

Sometimes the surface we see has a pattern; you see a visual pattern.

They are everywhere, in every which way. It's best to simply see examples. But we can tell you this— in its simplest definition, pattern is the repetition of visual surface forms.

Sometimes patterns show up as light and shadow. A pattern can also be a strong color image. In part, that is why it is introduced at this stage of the training. At this stage, it's fine if your pattern blend in forms from other assignments. It is the nature of pattern to occur with the other forms. You have likely shot some strong pattern pictures already.

Some patterns break the pattern, what we call *random patterns*—the way gold maple leaves scatter on an asphalt surface or the tangled display of ribbons of many colors in a storefront window.

Patterns, both regular and random, are a feature of the natural world, like a row of trees. But pattern is far more pervasive in urban lives, such as rows of bricks on a wall. In the pattern assignment, your possibilities are almost limitless.

It's time to take an adventure in what you see and the way you see. This assignment is as much about your way of seeing as it is about a form of the phenomenal world, which makes this assignment fun and creative. You have free rein to play with the visual world.

But then, this is true of every assignment. Every assignment, every perception, and every equivalent image is a mirror of your practice and your way of seeing. This is the nature of deep contemplative practice. Pattern exploration is just more fun and easy and obvious. Which is its own lesson: the contemplative way is as straightforward and fun as it is deep and profound.

The pattern assignment and exploration is wide-open. Enjoy it!

In these example pattern shots, you can see that pattern can be quite regular, as in the first two photographs, or a little less so, as in the last. Color and light tend to also appear in pattern pictures. Remember that it is rare to get a level one shot that is "just the assignment"—the phenomenal world does not know or care about our assignments! Simply set your dial to noticing and filling your frame with the wild diversity of pattern out there.

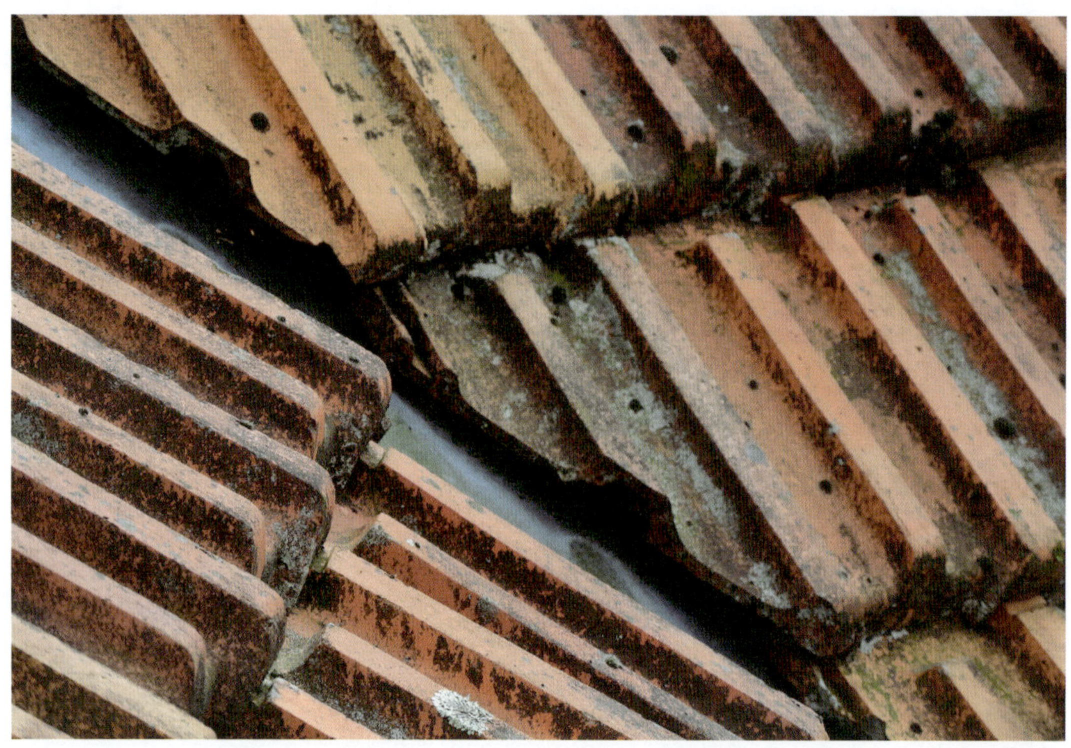

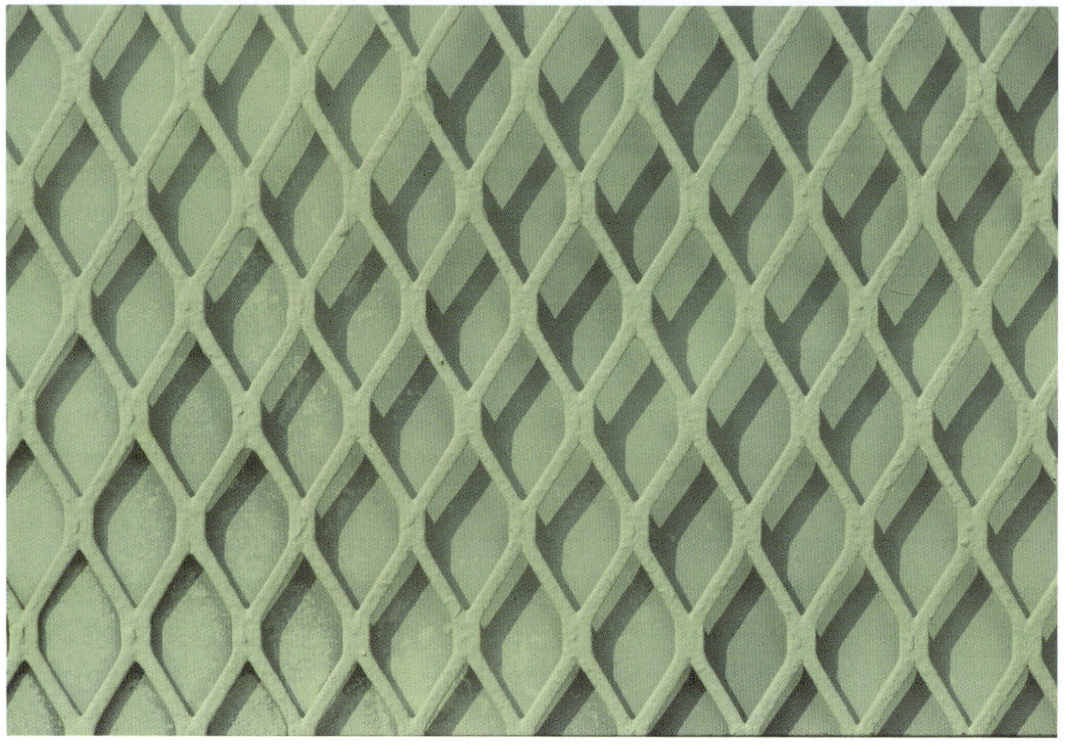

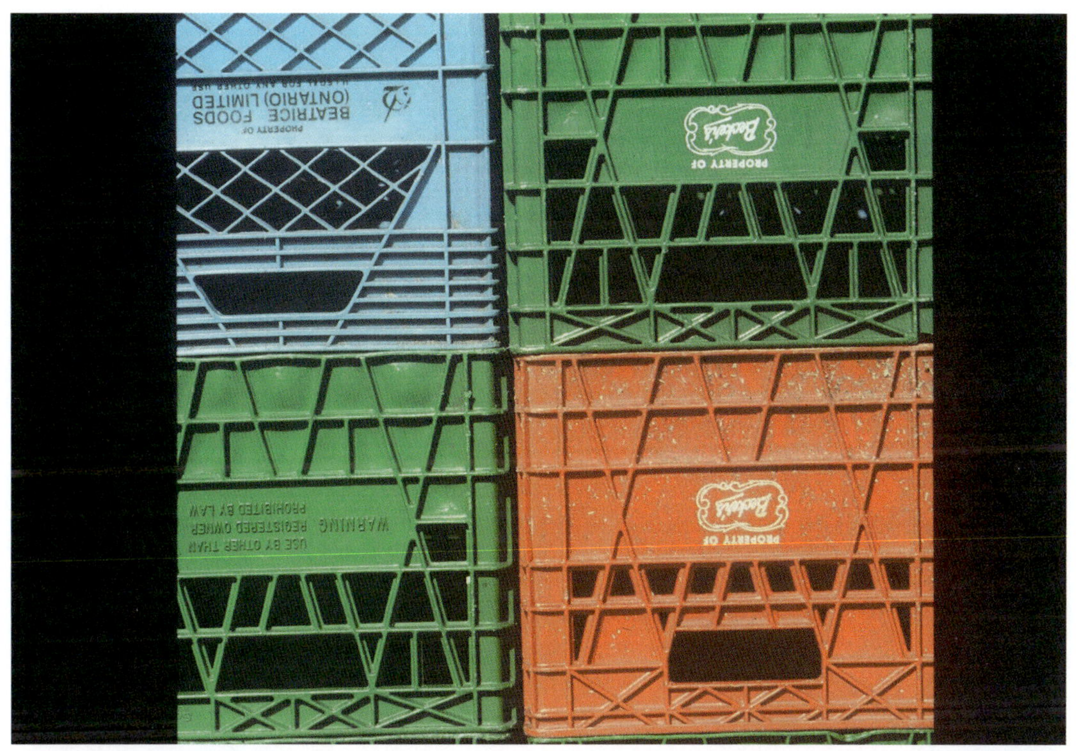

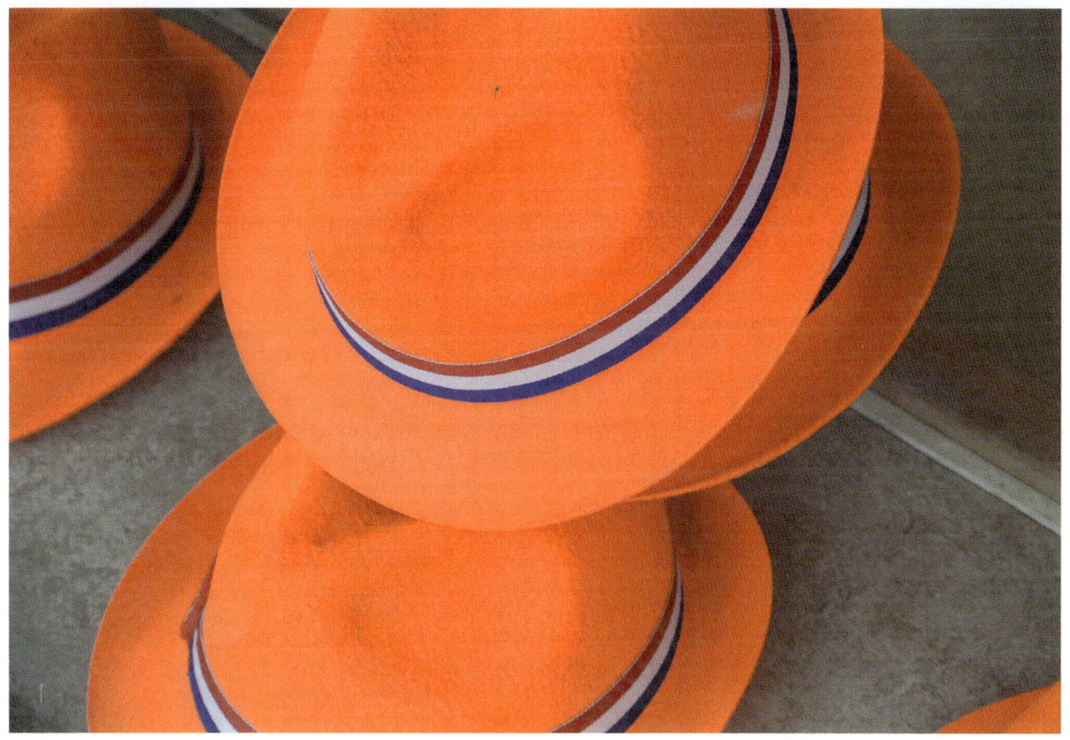

SECTION SIX:

VIEW INTERLUDE

CONTEMPLATIVE RECOLLECTION

Having completed these assignments, it is good to pause and recollect what you have learned—not so much what you have learned about color, light, texture, and pattern, but the general contemplative lessons.

These lessons translate to your whole life; they *transform* your whole life. To be contemplative is to appreciate your life in a direct way. (Again, if you feel so inclined, you can postpone this section and move on to the final level one assignments: Space and Dot in Space.)

Each moment presents the opportunity to wake up to our life by tuning in with our sense perceptions: to really taste our food, for example, or to hear the sound of thunder. When my father moved to the West, he noticed that sometimes we think that in order to be "spiritual," we need to shut down our sense perceptions. He said, "We feel we have to convert them into some sort of mythical idea of what things should be like." When we shut down our sense perceptions, we grow numb to our natural energy and disengage from our life. We tend to become heady—intellectually and emotionally isolated from the environment—and we lose the capacity to feel. Without feeling, we are no longer fully being on this planet, because we have lost the capacity to care. This is how kindness and compassion start to wane. To proceed down this road is a tragedy of astronomical proportions. My father said, "Any perception can connect us to reality properly and fully." Now announces itself through our sense of touch, taste, sight, sound, and smell. What are you smelling right now? When we appreciate our senses fully, this is the moment when goodness is being expressed. Each moment feels fresh: We connect with how things are. Red is red, and a racehorse is a racehorse. We have heard about basic goodness, but after encountering it viscerally, we feel that it is true.

—Sakyong Mipham, *The Shambhala Principle*

THE FLASH OF PERCEPTION AND THE PURE PERCEPTION

It is worth contemplating the experience of the flash of perception further, before engaging the Dot in Space assignment. As you will see, the flash of perception is directly related to the visual element of dot in space.

Do not get fixated on the word *flash*. It can be expressed in many ways: gap, shift, jolt, jerk, opening, and so forth. Notice how most of these expressions are physical—staying connected to the physical experience of the flash of perception is vital.

Flash of perception is one of the keys to Nalanda Miksang practice. You might want to try the flash of perception exercise for a brief period as a refresher. In any case, definitely bring to mind your direct experience(s) of the flash of perception.

Consider:

1. The flash of perception is somewhat unconditional.

2. We experience it as a gap in the stream of conventional experience.

3. The flash of perception opens perception itself.

Recall that when you look and see in an intentional way, you become synchronized. For example, when you intend to see color as color, you perceive color. Anytime you experience a flash of perception, the perception comes to you. It happens before you have a thought about it, long before you have an interpretation. It comes out of the blue, out of who knows where or why. It just comes.

In this sense, it is unconditional. It does not come from you and your interpretations, or even your contemplative intentions. It exists before and beyond these.

In effect, it comes from the phenomenal world. In this practice, we are letting the world make the first move. This is the direct Way of deep receptivity, which is a positive way of saying nonaggression, of being open to possibilities and spontaneity. This is deep contemplative practice; this is ordinary magic.

The flash of perception appears as a surprise, fresh and startling. It stops the eye and stops the mind. It issues as a gap, a suspension, and an opening. It suspends the flow of the conventional stream of experience. Suddenly there is *that*. It even suspends your contemplative intention. Become familiar with that gap: it is a key to the whole path of Nalanda Miksang.

At this point, you probably mainly experience the gap as a break in your conventional stream of experience. From our conditional or habitual situation, this makes sense. This is a good thing: it radically shifts the possibilities of our regular points of view. Already, this is the contemplative Way of living. It is good to know and experience the now very suddenly; we can shift beyond our habitual ways into fresh and unexpected ways.

However, this gap runs much deeper. To start to have a sense of its depth, try to let go of the idea of this gap as a suspension within an ongoing conventional stream of experience. Think of it instead as a kind of ongoing opening of *experience itself.* Abstract philosophy? Maybe. But it is also direct and practical advice: we are alive and our life is a life of experience and perception.

A traditional meditation analogy is that we experience the gap of perception like a gap in a cloudbank, which lets the sun shine through. For a moment, we glimpse the vision of the clear, blue sky. The absolute reality, however, is that the sun is always shining. The sky is always the whole vast blue space. In other words, what we experience as a gap is just a gap in our relative experience. In an ultimate sense, the gap is actually reality peeking through our struggle to say hello.

What the flash of perception opens is perception itself. If you can be present to the flash, if you can be with the happening as it happens, an opening comes toward you and recedes and moves away. It comes toward you as seeing and moves away to be *that color.* It establishes the perception poles of the perceiver and the perceived. This is a nondualistic experience of dualism.

When we say that the flash of perception does not come from you, but rather from other, we do not mean that it comes from outside, from some "other" in that sense. Rather, it exists before the separation of *self* and *other,* perceiver and perceived. It exists before dualism. This points to a profound feature of being alive: we are part of a larger, interdependent circuit of being. We are not and can never be separate from all that is. We have a basic and trustworthy connection to things as they are. When we say that the flash of perception opens to perception itself, we mean a direct experience of this truth. Even if the moment seems fleeting, the truth is not.

The phrase *flash of perception* suggests that it is a fleeting experience. It is not. A flash of perception does not happen in clock time. In it, we experience a timeless moment. So the problem is not remembering it or grasping it. The issue is a matter of staying with it, becoming familiar with it.

Why is this possible? Because at the heart of the flash of perception, there is a tremendous stillness. Conventional time is suspended. Perception opens. The gap is not vacant nor a vacuum. It is full of stillness and a vibrant clarity.

You cannot measure or grasp this in time itself. But you can feel it in experience. Your eye and mind are held in this suspension. You can abide in this still and timeless moment.

Another way of saying this is that we can rest in the moment of *nowness.* There is no other now than this now. The flash of perception and the experience of nowness are Ways of the same reality. They manifest the same qualities of calm abiding, openness, and being fully present. The orientation to the mind of nowness is also the Way of the meditation disciplines. This is one place where contemplative practices and meditation converge.

WORKING WITH THE FLASH OF PERCEPTION

The qualities of the flash of perception are the qualities of the contemplative experience and mind. Contemplating this may help you to recognize such openings when they occur. They occur all the time, but we seldom give them the attention they deserve. Clear seeing is not something you create: it the basic resource. It is something that you realize.

Our approach is based on what Chögyam Trungpa calls *true perception*. *True Perception* is the title of his book on contemplative dharma art. Sometimes we use the expression *clear seeing* or *pure perception*. These terms are equivalent expressions.

The basic view and approach is twofold: true perception and basic goodness. And the Way of ways.

Nalanda Miksang holds that true perception is isomorphic or resonant with basic goodness. It also holds that true perception is a practical embodiment, expression, and celebration of this basic goodness. Basic goodness is the reality and proclamation that our lives, through all their ups and downs, are worth living because life is intrinsically worthwhile. It has intrinsic value. And we can connect with and appreciate this goodness. Appreciating this intrinsic value both affirms and increases it, so we can simultaneously affirm and increase the value or meaning of our lives.

Nalanda Miksang is informed by various Eastern contemplative traditions which hold that we experience the phenomenal world—or what in the Daoist language they call the "ten thousand things"—in all of its complexity through the simple-seeming patterns of our daily situation.

The background of Nalanda Miksang includes these teachings. But our approach is more direct and conventional. We just work with experience of the visual as the visual. Our first investigation is very simple, direct, and ordinary: What is the visual, and how can we make contact with it? How can we express this as photographic images, so for instance, color as color, red as that just so/just that red?

It is that simple and that profound. In making direct contact with red, we also experience what it is like to make contact with the phenomenal world, and with the basic wisdom of this manifestation.

These moments cut through the many obstacles to clear seeing: preoccupations, preconceptions, preferences, story lines, beliefs, and so forth. These pure perceptions exist outside that whole system of filters and distortions. You can begin to distinguish the open quality of clear seeing from the self-enclosed cocoon of habitual frameworks.

Notice how this works in practice. You have a flash of perception—red! Your eye and mind stop. Your thoughts halt. Lifted out of your comfort zone, you feel the shock of a penetrating perception. Your eye and mind identify with or are absorbed by that perception. You are completely present with and held by that perception. Finally, you feel a deep sense of stillness, space, and stability.

The gap is really the breakthrough of birthright wholeness and goodness. These affirmative qualities are described as the five wisdoms. These wisdoms are not esoteric or external; they are the inherent awake qualities of your mind, heart, and life. The pure perceptions and the equivalent images embody these "awake" qualities.

The Way of synchronization and Way of the flash of perception are two sides of the same reality: pure perception. The flash of perception delivers a pure perception. With that pure perception, your eye mind and the phenomenal world are in the same place at the same time; they are synchronized and aligned—harmonized.

You cannot force a flash of perception to happen. But you can solicit one. Synchronization establishes the conditions that transmit the unconditioned. Nalanda Miksang synchronization—view, motivation, intention, and so forth—creates a contemplative lightning rod for the flash.

The practice of synchronization also channels that flash in creative and enlightening ways. Through synchronization, sight becomes insight, then images, and then insightful images.

Therefore, we need both the flash of perception and synchronization of perception: they work together as one in the practice of the Way of Seeing.

DEEP FEATURES OF THE FLASH OF PERCEPTION

It is worth exploring the qualities of the flash of perception because they are also qualities of contemplative mind, otherwise called the *mind of nowness.*

A flash of perception happens. A distinct perception suddenly opens. The ongoing flow of conventional experience breaks, allowing a breakthrough. Even the intent of clear seeing as a preoccupation breaks—and suddenly you are there with *that*: that color, that texture, etc. It is not something that you can gradually bring into place or that you can control as an outcome. You can anticipate it, but it will always arrive its own way.

The contemplative mind orients to this "other," to that which comes in its own way. It is a difference that makes a difference. Opening through the gap, the contemplative mind arrives, fresh and free. This flash or gap can feel like shock. Its main feature is the shock of reality—the shock of ordinary reality, the shock of experiencing ordinary, everyday perception as reality. The shock of discovering where you have already always been living. Contemplative mind experiences this shock, this sudden wake up to ordinary reality.

We experience it as coming from other, but not from outside. It is automatically free of self-preoccupation. It is pure perception. Therefore, contemplative mind is free from self-preoccupation and connects with pure perception. Contemplative mind *is* the shock of connecting with the ordinary reality that is our birthright.

There is no doubt. Contemplative mind is, to use Chögyam Trungpa's famous phrase, "First thought, best thought."

At first, this flash may seem disorienting. It may feel overwhelming. We are used to shutting out a lot of the world around us. You may feel ambushed by no longer being in your comfort zone, no longer working with your conventional reference points, and no longer working with your filters, story lines, and context.

Contemplative mind is not always what we think it will be or what we want it to be. Some people have a concept that contemplative mind will be peaceful. Actually, it involves traveling a real path of transformation. In order to reorient, first it disorients us.

The flash of perception has no external context; it is free and a free-for-all. Entering this free-for-all, the eye and mind fall through the phenomenal world. This is terrifying when we fight it. However, it is exhilarating when we relax into it.

In the contemplative approach, we can have our cake and eat it too. We can discover a different, a more effective form of peace: nonstruggle or, even better than nonstruggle, a liberated free fall.

The contemplative mind is adventure and exhilaration.

Don't worry. It may be free from habitual association, but pure perception has its own internal integrity. The eye and mind stop and synchronize. They gather in the present moment of nowness. Freed from habitual projection, pure manifestation is possible. This is what is meant by *purity*. The pure present moment will never drop you.

Being gathered as the present moment, we can identify *with* the present moment. This is the experience of nondualism. We can experience being absorbed by or yoked to the present moment, not in bondage but in deep communion. We are not one—it is not an act of dissolving into something. But we are also not two—there is no separation. Instead, the contemplative mind is communion, contact, and connection. We connect with the connection. We feel one pointed but at ease, alert but relaxed, disoriented from our ordinary experience but oriented in the reality of the moment.

As you experience even a glimpse of this free fall, it is important to note that the gap of perception is not a vacuum. It is not nothing; it is the complete just that/just so of just this nowness. It is like riding a wave. It is surfing the timeless now moment. It has the quality of being buoyant. As mind and eye surf in the present moment, the contemplative mind feels powerful and joyful. You feel empowered and joyful. You see the truth of the phenomenal world. Looking becomes seeing. Sight becomes insight.

The structure of practice—assignments, forms, etc.—all help to leverage us closer to these insights. Contemplative mind creates images that communicate these insights.

THE GAP OF PERCEPTION AND THE FIVE WISDOMS

Let's return to this idea from the last section: the gap of perception is not empty. It is a plenitude of elements. In Tibetan meditation traditions, these essential qualities of the phenomenal world are called *the five wisdoms.*

This is a deep teaching Nalanda Miksang presents at the end of the path of training. Chögyam Trungpa also presents these teachings after the Three Levels of Perception. But these wisdoms subtly manifest in the flash of perception, even in the beginning. So it's time to present their pith characteristics. These five wisdoms are: space and equality; clarity; richness; attraction, beauty, and harmony; and dynamic energy.

SPACE AND EQUALITY

Space and equality suggest that the flash of perception is a sense of openness. There is nothing missing and nothing to add. There is a sense of completion. There is no need, and indeed no real possibility, of further interpretations. Just that/just so, just now.

Also, no single special perception exists. Each perception is the manifestation of things as they are—each pure perception, each equally special.

Images are still and unique because they are made from the Way of clear perception. The Way itself is based in stillness, duration, and equanimity.

CLARITY

Clarity suggests that when you see things as they are, what you see is accurate and clear, sharp and brilliant.

In this open space, there are no obscurations. In this space of clarity, you see clearly. You have no doubt that you are seeing what you see. There is no second guessing or need for second-guessing. You are precise and confident.

As well, the phenomenal world itself seems transformed—free of your conceptual filters, it shines. Of course, what we are really clearing is your eye. At times, we have thought another translation for Miksang could be not just *good eye* but *clear eye.* In this brilliance, we can see what was there all along—the phenomenal world is precise and articulated. Each detail is already there and clear, definite.

RICHNESS

A related quality is richness. The awake, phenomenal world is not only clear and brilliant; it is also very rich. A directly perceived red has its own hue, tonal value, and saturation. This is the richness of things as they are.

This richness also enriches you. You feel completely satisfied and fulfilled with this complete perception. The images are a visual feast, a delight to appreciate.

ATTRACTION, BEAUTY, AND HARMONY

Already, in perceiving purely, you are attracted. As with most situations involving attraction, it is almost always too late before you realize it. You are already there—by the time you notice your flash of perception, you're already seduced, an interest and a connection already exists.

This is the deep quality of attraction. It is not just an intellectual or photographic experience. It runs more deeper and directly. The flash of perception excites us. It is that simple and that profound. Where there is pure perception, there is pure passion.

Let's examine the perception quality of attraction.

We are attracted by what is attractive. Based on our conceptual, conventional, and personal notions of what is attractive, we tend to make distinctions between what is beautiful and what is not beautiful.

Direct perception escapes such distinctions. We encounter beauty beyond and before our conventional categories. Pure perception reveals the inherent beauty of anything—rotting leaves, cigarette butts, dead birds, etc. Content is beside the point. The pure beauty of reality attracts us passionately.

It is difficult to find a word for this inherent beauty. It includes the other qualities of space and equality, clarity and brilliance, and richness. A better word might be *harmony*, if we understand harmony as meaning "completely together." In passion, we find ourselves together. We are not two. It is a form of union, sometimes of ecstasy, so it is a passionate harmony.

Harmony reflects another quality of pure perception: synchronization. When eye, mind and phenomenal world are in the same place, we tap into the joy of experience. Again, this experience may not be conceptually beautiful. It is always vivid.

At a personal level, this attraction to spontaneous beauty is what helps sustain us in this practice of making images. The experience is beautiful. The images are beautiful. Sharing the images is beautiful. All that is beautiful. So we enter the practice of passion, the practice of unbiased joy and beauty.

Harmony is the resonance of synchronization: all parts work together to create the whole. In this case, the whole is the passion of pure perception. It is not philosophical. It is the intense sense of being together in passion.

DYNAMIC ENERGY

How does synchronization happen?

We do not have to figure it out. A feature of pure perception is that it always already works. This is what basic goodness actually means—not just enough but plenty, always. That is all you need to know. That is all you need to do.

Take this as your mantra: as it is, it works.

Pure perception holds the details together, and the details are more than connected: they actively conduct the flow of connection. Formally, the aspects are in dynamic harmony.

Stopped by a pure perception, we feel this energy. It is not just an aesthetic. It is lively, life itself, inherently dynamic.

In practical terms, this is how perceptions provide natural composition. We feel where the perceptual action is, where the focal point is and where the supporting elements are. We do not have to figure out the image composition, because as pure perception, it is already dynamic. From this natural situation, we make contemplative images.

A natural, dynamic composition gives images more power. That power communicates with the five wisdoms of pure perception: space, clarity, richness, attraction, and dynamic energy.

HOT BOREDOM AND COOL BOREDOM IN CONTEMPLATIVE PHOTOGRAPHY

Meditation is one of those words, like *love*, that can have many meanings for many people in different contexts. In Shambhala Buddha dharma, meditation is a translation of the Tibetan word *gom*, "to become familiar." Meditation practice is a way to become familiar with things as they are. That includes both familiarities with the phenomenal world and with oneself. This familiarizing is Nalanda Miksang practice too.

In meditation, the mirror of your mind often reveals the endlessly mundane and conflicting contents of your ongoing preoccupations. This becomes a bit much, possibly even claustrophobic. Is this really the tranquility you hoped for when you started meditating? Shambhala teachings call this itchy, awkward place of having our faces crammed up into our own stuff *hot boredom*. Many people stop meditating when they reach this point. But the main idea is to go beyond this. Why?

Our discursive, chatty minds and the stories we tell ourselves are only the surface of things as they are. We say we come seeking peace, but it turns out we were seeking escape. Don't escape. Stay put and work through it, and you can arrive at cool boredom.

Cool boredom involves letting go of expectations, working with what happens as it happens. With cool boredom, you let go, relax, and open.

Chögyam Trungpa describes cool boredom as a stream that flows over and accommodates many features: rocks, vegetation, and so forth. It feels like a mountain river, flowing with freshness, harmony, and curiosity. Does that sound boring? What's "boring" is that it is now. The only now is now. There is nothing to add or take away. Feeling complete and present is the result of cool boredom.

The other "boring" aspect is that it is ordinary. It is not special or different from our ongoing lives. It is not external entertainment. It is simply living. But suddenly we appreciate that living, and ordinary magic arrives into the space our appreciation makes.

This is meditation. Contemplative photography is more focused. It focuses on visual pure perception and equivalent images, but the process is similar. Here's how those same teachings translate to Nalanda Miksang practice.

At first contact with Nalanda Miksang, many people are exhilarated. They contact fresh perception, and they become brilliant photographic artists. Then, some of them become bored. There is no end to having clear perceptions, no end of brilliant equivalent images. No image is the *ultimate* special image.

What could be construed as richness—the endless manifestation of clear perceptions and brilliant images—becomes a bore. They want to be special, creative, known for making special, creative images.

So they grasp for other photographic means, trying to stay entertained, trying to find that one special photo. Just to be clear, nothing is intrinsically wrong with technological explorations.

However, these subtle desires can keep us from going deeper, from completely opening to the contemplative way. They can become hot boredom.

The level one teachings open a fresh and direct Way. But we can settle into that as a new comfort zone. To stay connected to the depthless depth, to open the possibilities of ordinary magic, we can't get too comfortable with the practice.

Looking and contemplative experience is not enough. At some point, they too can become habitual. Even if it is fun and fresh to make brilliant images, in the long run, it loses its charm. Losing momentum is an indicator that you are still closed to the forward vision of the endless possibilities of possibilities.

The real practice is your own transformation. The real journey happens through insight into how to live your own deeply fulfilling, contemplative Way.

Stay with the fresh, endless possibilities of perception, with the insights you gather there continuously. Although it is always perception, it is never the same old, same old.

Like mountain spring water, cool boredom is deeply refreshing.

A NOTE ON HEARTBREAK

As Pema Chödrön notes, you must start where you are. One cannot begin with the fantasy of "harmonization," "peace," and " brilliant images." We cannot begin with artistic and spiritual fantasy. We must begin with our honest and experienced sense of the separation between the perceiver and the perceived, our sense of "self" and our sense of "world." The path to such realization must work through both these poles of conventional perception.

As perceivers, our sense of perception is often filtered, our versions of things as they are, are distorted by the needs of the ego.

In general, we struggle with two main filters or points of reference. Our main reference point is our strong sense of separation between the perceiver and the perceived. If we are honest, we acknowledge a strong conviction that we really exist as substantively *here* and that the world really exists as substantively *there*—and further, that the world that is *there* is a world full of *things*. The world is a kind of container for things: chairs, rooms, houses, streets, cities, land, trees, sky, sun, moon, stars…it goes on and on.

Personally, we may feel somewhat separate. The contemplative practice both honors and transcends that sense of separateness. The contemplative view and Way is that we are unique and, therefore, in a certain sense, alone. But it stresses that we are also unique and alone *together*, so we can share and celebrate this common circumstance.

The second main filter includes the various views, opinions, emotions, and active strategies we engage in concerning the world that is *there.*

In general, given our sense of a split between *the world, and us* we adopt three formal strategies: attraction (we like, want, desire, seduce, celebrate, etc.); repulsion (we deny, reject, turn away, push away, destroy, etc.); or ignorance or sitting on the fence (we are disinterested, indifferent, look away, ignore or gloss over, etc.). We are constantly engaged in trying to get ourselves and our situation "together"—trying to get both together simultaneously. This is mostly a struggle. We are not easy; we are not at ease.

The Nalanda Miksang practice of purification and harmonization helps put us at ease. We start with making direct and pure contact with the visual world as the visual world, with the visual world as a phenomenal display we can experience through color, light, and so on. We start with making contact with this pure or true perception.

Then, as perceivers, we "bracket," or take out of play or put on hold, our particular complexes, interpretative filters, or preconceptions. In more affirmative terms, we experience the reality of contact, communion, and communication.

Contact provides a moment of nondualism, just being there with the *there.* In retrospect, it feels synchronized and complete. At the time, we more or less disappear. No longer self-conscious, we are "red as red" or "shadow as shadow." This may feel liberating, exhilarating, like a sort of free fall, or it may feel less dramatic, like a sort of suspension as though we are hanging in with the hanging out—or hanging out with the hanging in. Actually, this suspension is the more mature contemplative way.

Communion offers a sense of getting it in a nonconceptual way. We feel a deep sensibility and understanding without being able to say it in so many words or so many images. We are in touch and are touched. The heart of all contemplative practices is this communion of touch.

This is also the heartbreak of all contemplative practices. It cannot be fully communicated. Even the initial communication is not complete. If we are clear and honest, we acknowledge there is always a gap. This simultaneous heart connection and heartbreak is the heartbeat of the contemplative way.

Chögyam Trungpa is quite clear on this point. He compares the experience to unrequited love. The experience is one of genuine sadness. The fulfilled communion cannot be completely fulfilled nor fully communicated. It is too deep, too enriched, too personal, and too intimate—also too direct and too ordinary.

Does this correspond to your conceptual hopes? To your ambitions for artistic accomplishment and contemplative peace? To your desire that you and your art image will be victorious, setting a new standard for brilliant images? To your yearning for this dharma practice to finally give you peace? Dharma teachings say this is an unrealizable fantasy. You might get some short-term social confirmation…but then you die.

The contemplatives have a different view of "victory." One actually realizes life as life, sees things as they are, and makes a heart connection with the unceasing display and the unaccountable richness of the radiant phenomenal world.

This experience is neither mystical nor unavailable. On the contrary, our endlessly unrequited love is the only indirect and affirmative way to the Way. It is what we achieve in making contact with a clear perception and making an equivalent image.

The power of the gap means that the participants who view these equivalents are free to experience their own contact, connection, and communication beyond your image. By connecting with the image, finding inspiration through the image, and developing insight through the image, they become participants in it. From the first perception to the communal reception, communion is possible.

Making a strong and vivid image becomes an inspiration. It is magic. It opens a powerful vector of communion with that which cannot be fully communicated.

So it is not just your adventure, your transformation, and your images anymore. The images communicate contact and communion. And they have their own life beyond your personal experience. They open to the world and the world opens to them. Here is a deeper view of Nalanda Miksang contemplative practice: it is an opening to the general good of a good society.

FINAL LEVEL ONE ASSIGNMENTS — SPACE and DOT in SPACE

Space and Dot in Space are the two final assignments of Nalanda Miksang level one. They are culminating assignments, both in difficulty and in profundity. In the usual course, after color, light and surface, space is the next assignment and then dot in space.

But some people find photographing space very difficult. It's hard to get hold of visual space. It seems elusive. Though we are working with space as purely visual, the topic invites concepts about space as an idea. So start with the space assignment, but if you find it gives you a headache, take a break. Move on to dot in space. You can always return to space later, or you can alternate between space and dot in space.

Each naturally illuminates the other. Space as a visual element does not stand on its own. It is a feature of dot in space, which is the form of perception itself.

INTRODUCTION TO SPACE

Visual space is one of the basic elements of seeing. Indeed, one of its features is that it is visually pervasive. It is everywhere and nowhere. As a visual exploration, space is not inherently difficult but sometimes seems that way. The confusion comes from two directions: the variety of ways space can appear (our perceptions) and our contradictory understandings of space (our concepts).

In our experience, there are many ways to interact with space. For now, let's keep it simple and consider just two: the space we walk through and the space we see through. They are the same space, but we have different experiences of each.

Let's say you are sitting on one side of a room. On the other side, the room has a door. If you intend to go out that door, you have to walk through space to the door. It takes some effort, locomotion, and time. That's physical space.

Now say you are in the same room but only intend to *see* that door: you look, and you see it. Looking and seeing are almost effortless and instantaneous. That's visual space. To be totally clear, in contemplative photography, we work with visual space, not physical space. We often don't think of them as different, but they are.

In meditative and contemplative traditions, the idea of *space* is used as a teaching. In this context, the word points to an expansive way of being. Realization or enlightenment is presented in terms of embodied space. Both realization and space are boundless and all accommodating, for instance.

In Nalanda Miksang, we do not explore many ways or views of space. We simply focus on direct experience of visual space. The contemplative sensibility of space is there, but we relate to it physically, as a state of being.

We also view visual space in terms of perception.

The act of visually perceiving, of "seeing something," has a form. It is formally called *figure on a ground*. A good example is to think of what they call *negative space* and *positive space* in art. If you have a portrait, the head in the portrait is positive space and the negative space is whatever is not the head (the background or ground).

Nalanda Miksang's language for this relationship is *dot in space*, which comes from Chögyam Trungpa's teachings on the same. The background is space. However, what is background without a foreground? They always come together. That, together, is perception—seeing something in relation to something else.

In the space assignment, we actually try to see the background as the foreground, eliminating the dot or inverting it so the dot doesn't take up the foreground. When this occurs, space is experienced as a sustaining quality of the nature of perception. We so often focus on what is popping out from the background. Here, we become curious and open to the background itself.

SPACE ASSIGNMENT

Just as we work with color as color, here we work with space as space.

However, what is space as space? It helps if you don't approach space in these two habitual ways: 1) space as what is between things or 2) space as what surrounds things. These are misconceptions, because they are concepts. Neither describes the experience/perception of visual space *as* visual space. In fact, both confuse visual space with physical space. Both start with trying to find things and then trying to find visual space in relationship to a thing. Space is treated as the relationship between things or understood as something that is not a "thing." But we need to understand visual space on its own terms, as dynamic visual space with its own qualities.

In exploring visual space, it's vital to drop your orientation to things. So how do you start? In two related ways.

The first, seeing space as an element of the visual, is the outer way, the level one way. In this way, there is a little paradox—we assume the view of dot in space. Coming from this view, space is not something separate but part of the whole perception.

Here, you can still work with space as space, as simultaneously, you understand that space is the sustaining space where something is happening: a perception.

Here's how to understand this. Let's dip into dot in space a bit more.

When we see, we always see *something*. This is what we mean by dot in space on a perceptual level. Seeing something means that we see a foreground dot against a background space.

Because space is always a feature of dot in space, you cannot simply see or make an image of space. For example, an image of the clear, blue sky would not likely be a perception or an image of space. It might look somewhat blank and not very dynamic, but perception is always dynamic—indeed, perception is *that* dynamic. A reflected image of that sky might exhibit that dynamic more directly. A cloud in that sky would cause the sky itself to fall into the background of the cloud, which then becomes the foreground (the dot).

So here's the key: in shooting space, invert the relationship between the figure and the ground. Now the figure—the dot—serves as support for dynamic space. In effect, the dot becomes a supporting element. It recedes to the visual background, and the space element assumes the function of foreground.

In the exploration of making an equivalent image of space, there is always an aspect of the dot. In a dot-in-space image, the dot is the main focus. In a space image, the dot aspect becomes a minor player compared with space.

In terms of a pure space image, the dot usually, though not always, occupies an edge or corner of the image. It serves as an anchor or a diving board for the space. Sometimes the dot is more diffuse within the space. For example, in a water image, the trace of cloud formations or ripples or even tonal values can serve as a diffuse dot, subtly anchoring the space.

SUBTLETY OF SPACE

Trust your eye and mind, and the way the eye and mind work. Your attention wants to move off the support—what, if it stood out more, would be a dot—into the image, to a sense of space. Your attention, and that of your viewer, should stay and rest there. The result always lets the eye and mind rest in this element of space, rather than fixating on a foreground dot.

When viewing any image, but especially a space image, pay attention to how your eye and mind react. If one, your eye doesn't land somewhere, but instead, is buoyed by an overall space; and if two, your mind does not fixate somewhere but, at least initially, rests in a sense of expanse, then this is an equivalent image of space.

Both image and perception are lived and embodied. Allow yourself to experience space directly; then, communicate it so others can experience it directly.

The main practical point is that in space images, there is always a trace element of the co emergent dot, but the dot is not the focus. The focus, the foreground, is space.

Again, the main quality of visual space is that it is pervasive. It is tempting to think of space as a container of things. This is a wrong view. Visual space is not a container; it is a sustainer: it sustains the visual as the visual. It is a feature of the whole perception.

In the space assignment, you want to feel this quality of sustaining. In visual terms, the perception lacks a single visual focus, a dot in space. Yet, it isn't vacant; it has its own perceptual, sensible, and sensuous manifestation. It will be definite, sure, but without a single point of definition. We often call this a sense of overall-ness: a sustained, stable field of perception. This is the hallmark of the sensibility of visual space.

When you have a flash of perception of space, and when you observe a pure space image, your eyes should release and relax into to the image. No one point of focus holds your eye—that would be a dot in space—but you also aren't distracted or confused. Peace of mind, the *space* of mind, and space of image are in communion.

This space awareness is one of the key aspects of contemplative experience and aesthetics. Space is one of the elements of the visual, but it is also an element that pervades all the other visual elements, and it is a felt sensibility of the contemplative mind. It may seem as if we are referring only to one particular assignment, but the outer and inner qualities of space pervade all the assignments—they pervade the whole Nalanda Miksang practice.

Because the phenomenal world doesn't care about our levels, as you set your dial for space as an assignment, you will find yourself expressing it both in level one and level two ways.

In terms of level one, it is instructive to note the difference between a color image that manifests as color and a color image that manifests as space. The difference is both formal and experiential. In formal terms, it is an issue of what is in the background and what is in the foreground. However, most importantly, and easiest to understand, is the way the eye and mind synchronize with the image. Color is usually a definite and even dramatic perception. Bang! Color. No question. Sometimes it even has the sense of coming at you.

Space is subtler. There's no point of reference to stop the eye and stop the mind. Instead, your eyes relax into the overall-ness. The eye is gathered and the mind is still. So if an image has a lot of space, even if the perception was color, the color dissolves into the space.

Here we have a teaching concerning the phenomenal world: it is always a world of perception and never one of concepts. Even if a perception or shot has a lot of color, it may not be perceptually color. It may be space. Everything depends on the moment, the expression, the manifestation, and the perception.

These are level one experiences. Your exploration may open in a level two way. Often when people open up, they discover space as grand and obvious as a landscape setting, or the openness of a beach to the ocean and the sky, or the spaciousness of an urban facade's reflection, or even the intimate space of a room in your home.

For now, we open to space in a level one way, relaxed and abstract, and simply see what happens.

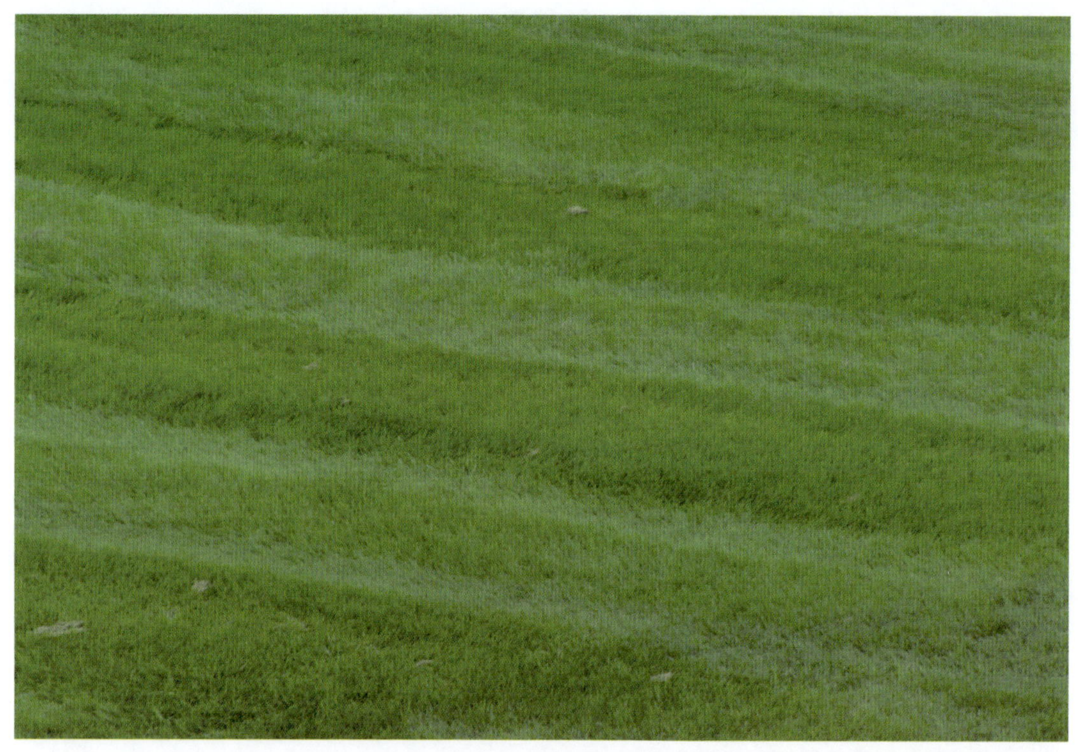

Remember that the experience in our space shoot is one of spaciousness—resting, opening, a lack of contrast. This is a visual experience that we feel as we look and See, and one we should make an equivalent of in our photograph. The first example is in water, an easy place to spot space. The second, however, is a bit of a car manifesting reflective space. The third example is grass, which can also be quite spacious, partially due to its overall tones. Finally, don't think there's no space in solid concrete or, in the case of the fourth photo, adobe.

ENDING THE SPACE ASSIGNMENT

Whether experienced in an abstract way or more recognizably in objects or situations, space is both nowhere and everywhere. Since it is everywhere, it is not a difficult assignment to perceive. It is only our anxiety and preconceived ideas that make space difficult to photograph. When we open space in our lives—like having a free weekend after a busy week—many experiences rush to fill the space. The same may happen with your perceptions in your practice, especially on your space shoot. Just relax and orient to space as the space of relaxation. Space is relaxation itself.

When I was younger, I worked in technical theater. While training as an actor, then as a technician and stage manager, many stage directors gave actors with bit parts this instruction: make sure you still have a motivation for your character. One director even told us that audiences could tell the quality of directing in a play or film not by how the main actors perform, but by how the background parts behave. If they look bored, as though they are just backdrop for the main action, that is a problem. They drain vitality from the main actors. If the background is too busy, it pulls attention from the main characters. Finding that balance is an unsung art in the directing world.

Now, whenever I watch a movie or play, I keep this in mind. It's such a part of my observing that I even take it into my life. At a café, at a rally, when teaching a class, I am watching for the person who either wishes to be or is forced into be in the background. I notice what she is doing, how she is interacting or not.

What goes on in what we call "the background" is a part of the whole, not something separate. The people who surround you in your life are not just "dressing"—they can make or break your ability to recover from a crisis, even help make for an enjoyable daily life—or not.

The same is true in visual perception. We often dismiss the full picture. Training in the space assignment helps us invert our looking just enough so we can start to see a more holistic balance. We begin to understand just how rich the whole phenomenal world is.

Dot in space is the central teaching of Nalanda Miksang. In fact, it is the source of contemplative aesthetics in general.

Like color, light, surface, and space, dot in space is yet another expression of the visual as the visual. In fact, it is the key to the visual as visual.

In the visual as the visual, the direct experience of perception, we always see something. That visual "something" could be color, light, etc. There is always a focal point where the eye stops and is held, where the visual is gathered. We do not just see in general; we always see *something*.

It could be anything, small or large—a mark on a wall, a light switch, a line in a poster or a single letter of that line, a saltshaker, a balloon, a gas station sign or just the curve of a gas station sign against the blue of the sky, a flower or the top petals of a flower, the stem of a flower, a dew drop on a leaf tip, a glass building against the sky, the moon, a face or eyes on a face…It goes on and on *because* it goes on and on in reality; there is no end to seeing something because seeing is always seeing *something*.

What does it mean to see *something*?

The answer can seem simple but very profound.

To use classic phenomenology terms, to see something is to see a figure on a ground. The figure grabs full attention, creating a foreground. The background is there but lacks the intensity.

In other words, we see one thing because it is not like what surrounds it.

As explained earlier, in art terms, this is called positive space (what we call dot/foreground) and negative space (what we call space/background). We see because of contrast. This is the structure or form of perception. Perception is not just seeing in general. Perception is seeing in this definite way through this foreground focus and a background context.

In other words, a perception is an expression of a foreground figure on a background. In our teachings, we call this dot in space.

We can see this in a classic optical illusion, which also turns out to be a very sound visual expression of the philosophy of perception itself: phenomenology.

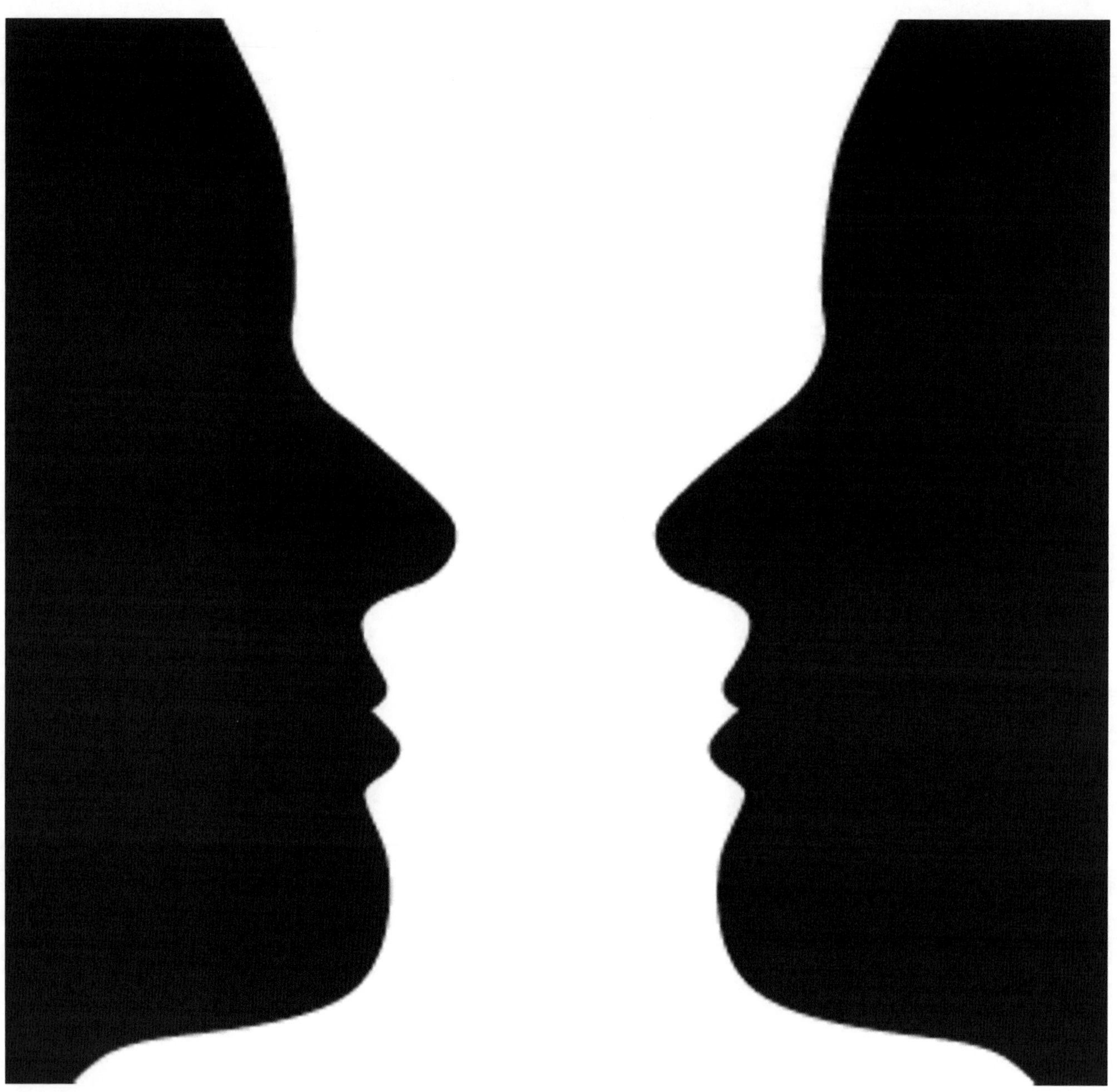

What do you see?

Some people see two faces. Some see a vase. You may see both, alternating. Theoretically, you cannot see both at once because the eye struggles to see only foreground without background and vice versa. We must have one to have the other. They coexist, but we can't see them both at once.

In lots of ways, we have already encountered this. When is a perception or photograph a patch of light? When is it a patch of shadow? It is actually a matter of which is perceived as foreground or background. It depends on the perceptual values. All perception works this way. For instance, in sound, you hear someone yell, a note play, or even the soft whisper of a fan because of the *not-that-sound* that surrounds it.

There are two lessons here. First, we always see something in particular against a more general background. Second, we help form that perception. The way we see either the vase or the faces in any given moment depends on how we are seeing it. The perceiver is always involved with the perceived and visa versa.

The implications are twofold. One, in terms of perception, there is no objective world to experience. Experience is this active forming of foreground focus and background context. Two, perceiver and the perceived are not truly separated. Perception is the communion of the perceiver and the perceived. They invite and complete one another.

The world is constantly shifting. In our optical illusion, there's both a vase and a face there all the time. Just because are view is shifting to only one at a time, it doesn't mean that's the only reality.

This may seem a little abstract. Here's what you want to remember: you are always connected and creative. In your ongoing, everyday life, you constantly fill in the blanks and connect the dots. You are an intimate part of an ongoing creativity. Your fundamental situation is creativity. You are a perpetual, natural artist. All you have to do is wake up and realize this. One way to realize this is to express it, and one of many ways to express it is Nalanda Miksang.

Doing so brings a sense of completion, harmony, and joy. This is the deep contemplative experience—connecting to reality through practice.

This is just a taste of the deep importance of dot in space—a taster of the deeper teachings. If your appetite is whetted, there will be more of those to come soon!

At this point, let's take a step back and keep it simple. For your assignment, just work with dot in space as a form of perception.

DOT IN SPACE ASSIGNMENT

The assignment is simple. See phenomenal manifestations, or things, as the form of dot in space. Make equivalent images. As always, the key is perception. We don't revert to conceptual or documentary photography.

For example, you may see and then make an image of a saltshaker. Rather than photographing things on a table, shoot from how they appear in phenomenal ways. All the phenomenal features we have explored so far—color, light, etc.—are in play. What you discover is that, in a way, all photographs we have taken so far are dot in space. There is a form to dot in space, and it starts to include all the other features we have explored. However, there is a simple joy to this direct contact and direct reality.

Dot in Space as Level One

Like our other assignments, the dot in space assignment easily slides from level one to level two expressions. To get a sense of the basic visual form, you can explore dot in space in a literal, level one way—a leaf on the ground, a splotch on a rug, a nail in the wall, a ball on the ground, etc. Your photographs will look abstract with little worldly context.

Even at its simplest, know that *dot in space* just means the perception of a figure on a background, not always a circle-shaped dot.

Nor does it have to be one dot; it can be many forms in a background space—a few stones on a sidewalk or a variation we call "sticks in sky": simple long forms, like urban light poles against sky. It's anything that demonstrates this basic perceptual visual form.

Taking this level one approach is good discipline. It may seem a bit simple, almost too easy, possibly even boring. However, it connects you with phenomenal perception. Be patient. This dot-in-space teaching reveals its depth over time, so it is good to work with simple perception first.

Again, dot in space doesn't always mean circle/dot shaped. We've included some very abstract/graphic examples. Some examples include the object-ness of the world and yet feel pretty abstract.

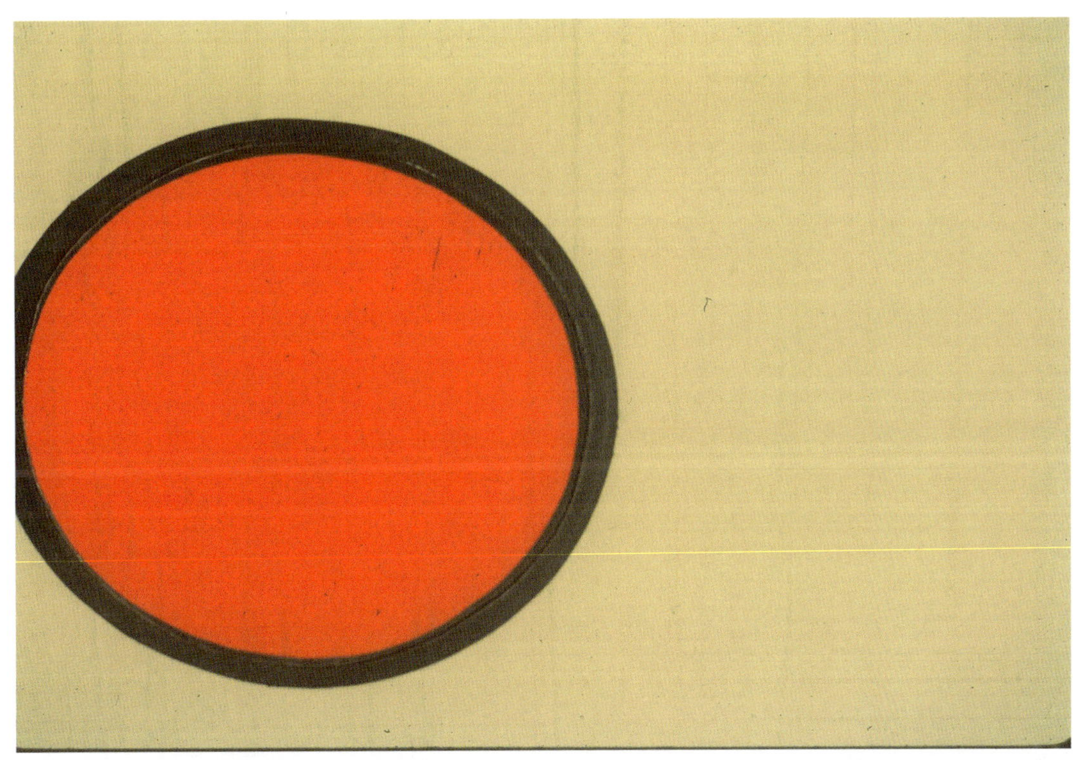

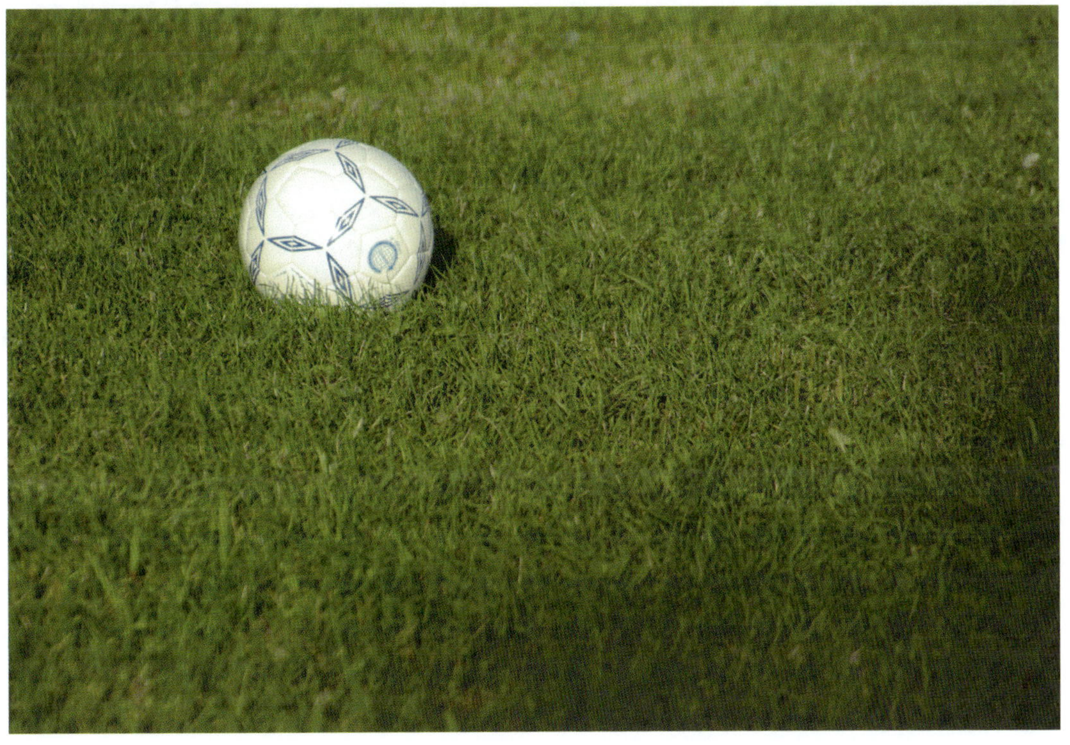

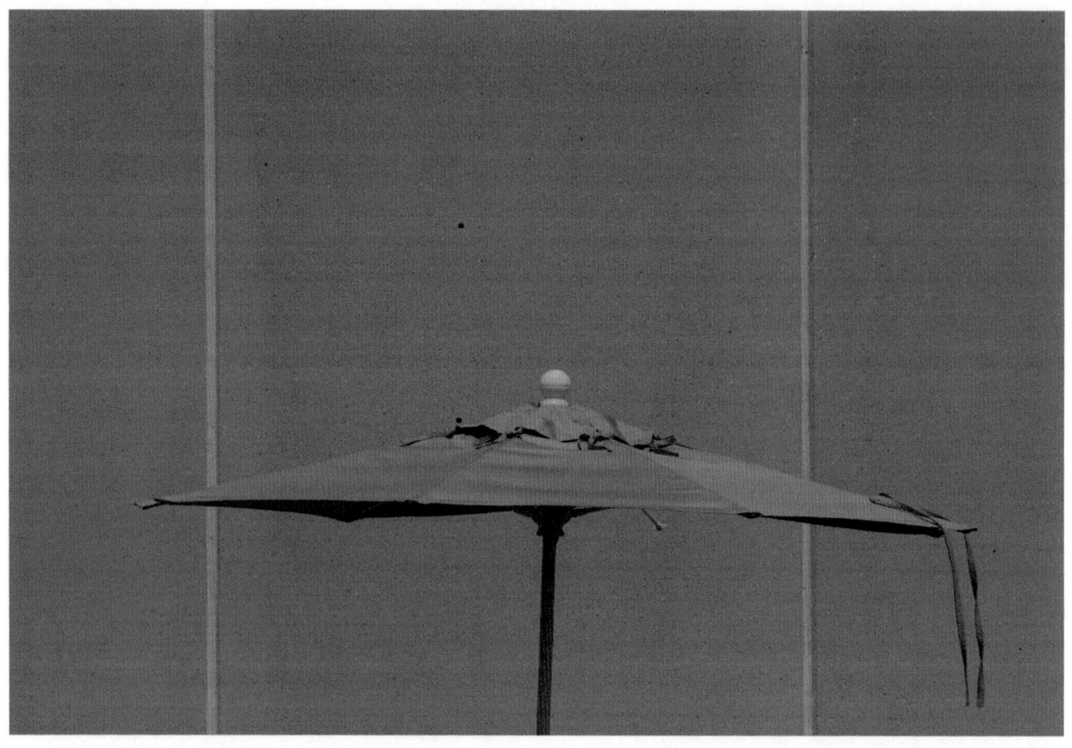

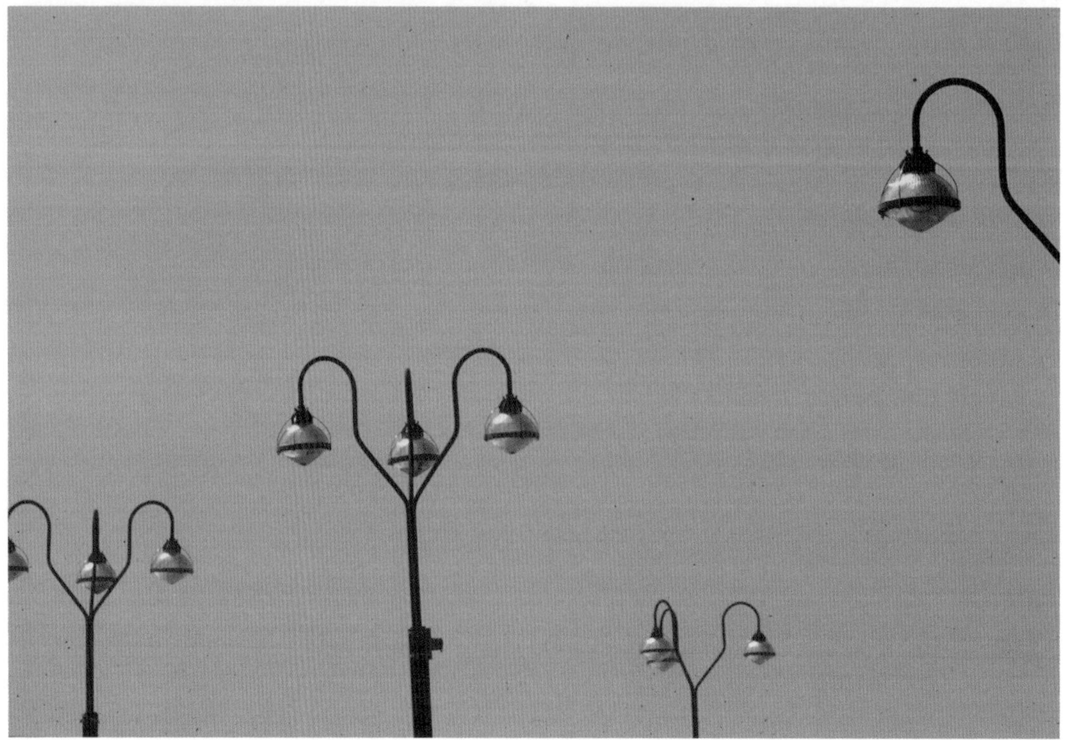

The first photograph is almost a joke dot in space it is so simple! We see how dot in space is actually how we saw color in the first place. In the second image, a dot in space is a bit more level two: we know what the object is, but it's the form of a shape against a background that is the core of the perception and image. Note that dot in space is not always circular. It is simply a color contrast or shape difference between foreground and background, which we can see in the umbrella image. In the lamp image, you can see how "dots" can repeat.

Dot in Space as Level Two

Nalanda Miksang's heart is the level two opening of the phenomenal world: the world of sense and sensibility, the world of ordinary magic and everyday beauty. Dot in space simultaneously reveals this resonance. It is the play of a surface and depth, or event and space. Dot in space reveals this as it moves from our simple level one experiences into the many expressions of level two.

Perception is more than a moment in time—it is a timeless moment. It is the whole perception. The whole perception is a vibration, and that vibration echoes and resounds. It is like a stone thrown into a still pond. It is like the simplicity of being there, like the still life paintings of the classic Dutch painters; it is the ordinary of ordinary magic. Like a still life, a level two dot-in-space image is no longer abstract. It is in the world with full heart. This is the timeless contemplative event and moment, as simple and profound as a heartbeat.

The deep sensibility of a perception, experience, and image is set in play. This feeling cannot be fully expressed. Nevertheless we express it; we make an image—a contemplative image. And that image transmits the resonance, so it goes on and on, beyond the event. Nalanda Miksang images open this heartfelt expression of this heartfelt response.

In the level two exploration, the resulting images are not abstract, like those of level one. They are recognizable things in their particular worldly context.

Though we are now exploring the world we experience—the world of things and contexts—we do not revert to a distanced documentation and representation. We stay in touch. We explore the perceived world, how the world of things manifests as a perception. As a perception, a thing manifests as the just-now phenomenal display: color, light, and so forth. More decisively, it manifests the communion of the perceiver and the perceived. This is not just a flower. It is the way aspects of that flower are perceived. Is it the fringe of top petals against the blue of sky? The elegant shape of the stems? The droop of one tulip petal and the feeling that it evokes? As perception goes, there is no such thing as a flower. There is no such thing as a thing. Perception goes on and on, but it is always just now. It is always the communion between you and the phenomenal world.

In this level two exploration, we allow content to manifest: the dot is no longer a formal perceptual value. Now it is a manifest reality—not a graphic form but a saltshaker. Not just any saltshaker, but *that* saltshaker in space. What you are photographing is your perception of that saltshaker in that moment in space. The subject of your photograph is your perception in that moment. This has always been the case but becomes even more important to notice in level two.

The background is also no longer a generalized formal space but a worldly context. In this particular exploration we engage and photograph the lived world, still staying within the parameters of this perceptual visual element and assignment.

So this is the assignment: explore the visual form of dot in space, but open up to a level two Way of Seeing. As you explored level one manifestations of dot in space, you likely stumbled into more level two images and perceptions. Discerning between the two is helpful in terms of a transition between level one and level two. Dot in space is the last assignment for level one and the first for level two. It bridges the eye and the heart.

In the review of the images, you should be able to distinguish the difference between the level one formal images and the level two resonant images. Transitional images happen, one that are not full one or two. Remember, the phenomenal world doesn't follow our rules. That's ok! The main point is to begin to exercise noticing the differences between the levels.

Here's what really makes level two dot-in-space images specific: they have an inner contemplative sensibility and aesthetic. Here, a picture is definitely worth a thousand words. So here are examples.

Feel the heart quality in these images. The first is a simple, spacious, and pure shot, with a strong Zen Aesthetic (a level two assignment) and also a Visual Haiku feeling (another level two assignment). In other words, not just dots in space and not just feathers. Then we can see how backlight really brings out a deep heartfelt quality in this leaf, the feeling of Visual Haiku: a tension of impermanence, the magic of a moment almost unseen.

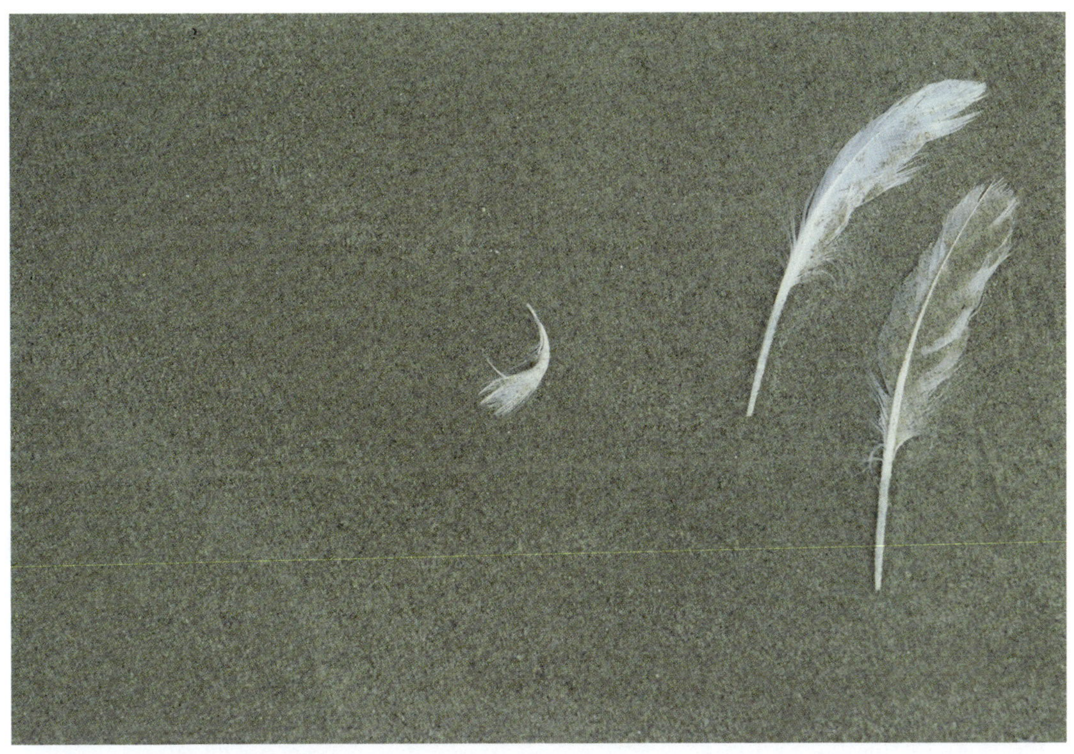

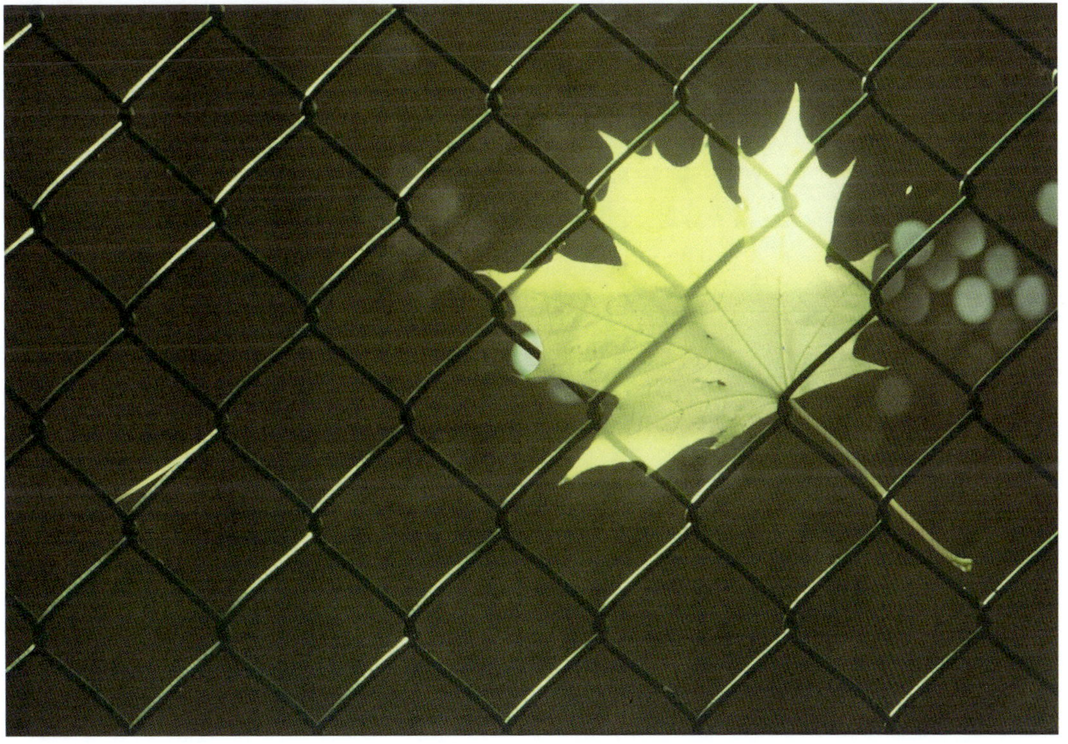

CLOSING THE LEVEL ONE ASSIGNMENTS

You have now completed all of the five assignments in level one Nalanda Miksang: Color as Color, Way of Light, Surface (Texture and Pattern), Space, and Dot in Space. In fact, there really is no "being done" with level one. Please keep this in mind as you read on into the deeper dot-in-space teachings in our last section.

SECTION EIGHT:

DEEPER DOT in SPACE

Any perception can connect us to reality properly and fully...there is some principle of magic in everything, some living quality. Something living, something real is taking place in everything...Drala could be called an entity...it is an individual strength that does exist...the discovery of drala, or magic, is indeed to establish your ties to the world so that each perception becomes unique...seeing one drop of water can be seeing all water...the dralas are elements of reality...anything that reminds you of the depth of perception...whatever is there, whatever you come across in your life, those are the dralas of reality. When you make that individual connection with the elemental quality of the world, you are meeting the dralas on the spot...the possibility of magic is always there.

—Chögyam Trungpa, *Shambhala Sacred Path of the Warrior*

DOT IN SPACE AND FIELDS OF PERCEPTION

Level two dot in space opens the whole of Nalanda Miksang exploration: the visual phenomenal world in its many dimensions. We will present this in a more complete way in the second book, *The Fields of Perception*. *Fields of perception* is a term from Chögyam Trungpa's Shambhala perception teaching. It points to the overlapping and interpenetrating dimensions of the phenomenal world.

Fields of perception, in terms of level two Nalanda Miksang, means the endless topic-oriented exploration of the phenomenal world. In level one, we explore based on basic visual forms. In level two, these forms relax, open up, and include the whole body of experience, the whole world. No longer just visual, the phenomenal experience is now heartfelt and plugs into the heartbeat of the world.

In the context of tying up level one and bridging to level two, dot in space is a form that can cut across and through the many fields of perception. A flower blossom level two dot in space can be simultaneous with a Flowers and Weeds (level two assignment) expression. A saltshaker can be a dot in space form in the Ordinary World (level two assignment) field of perception, and so on.

Dot in space is a feature of the basic visual constitution along with color, light, surface, and space. But it is also a framework that informs the overall perceptual exploration—the Way of seeing itself. With its resonant energy and great versatility, the ordinary dot is magic.

DOT IN SPACE, AUTHENTIC PRESENCE, AND THE NALANDA MIKSANG IMAGE

AUTHENTIC PRESENCE

In most Nalanda Miksang images, you find a lot of space. Why? Because we let the perception compose itself. In making a Nalanda Miksang image, we attend to the intrinsic nature of the perception—especially in level two, where something manifests as the way it is. It is not just a form. It is ketchup bottle in table space, or bee in flower space, whatever—but always a unique phenomenal *whatever*.

Why is it always in space? Well, it is not just in space. It has its own space: it radiates as a presence. Here we use a term from Chögyam Trungpa's Shambhala teachings. Everything has *authentic presence*.

Authentic presence is Chögyam Trungpa's translation of a Tibetan term *wangthang*, which means "field of power." In the Shambhala teachings, Chögyam Trungpa uses authentic presence to describe how a realized person manifests. People who are free of ego have a different feel about them; they are calmer but also expansive. That expansion is their authentic presence.

In pure perception, everything is free of ego. Everything radiates: rocks, flowers, and cats. This reality is connected to the teachings and reality of *drala*, or ordinary magic. We can see this in classical religious iconography, though it is present in everything.

Religions traditions, both Western and Eastern, share a common iconography: what we are calling authentic presence is symbolized with halos. Shambhala understands these to be symbols of authentic presence.

Not just saints manifest this radiance. You can discern it in everyday, ordinary things. Things have their own presence, their own space. Seen as phenomenal forms, through pure perception, they radiate a sensibility and space beyond the factual boundary of their forms. For a practical example, we could say that your body ends at your skin. Yet you are constantly shedding skin cells. Your body gives off a scent, and you make noise others can hear. So you are not just the seeming visual, or even physical, limit of your body.

Many artists have discerned this. For example, the paintings of Van Gogh express the energetic space between form and the space around it, whether stones, living beings, or bedroom furniture.

So when we make an image of a phenomenal form, a dot in space, the dot includes the intrinsic radiant space of (around) the phenomenal form. In making an image, we include that space. We give space to that dot in space. As a result, in its formal composition, the Nalanda Miksang image accommodates the space (or halo) around the phenomenal thing. It opens a lot of space. This is the principle of the formal composition: we do not just give space to the thing; we give space to its authentic presence.

This is not just a formality of composition. It is a deep contemplative inner teaching. The image's space is illuminated. Auspicious coincidence and authentic presence belong together. The unique constellation of aspects and elements that were there when you had your perception and took your shot are there in the image. Beyond the image, they also inform the unique radiance of living reality. It is difficult to express this in words. But this is what a Nalanda Miksang image transmits, regardless of content: articulate space—not spaced-out space, but the clear, direct, actual reality of space.

By *articulate space*, we mean that space is not just a formal value. Space is the way in which everything is interdependent. Here is a classic analogy: a butterfly halfway around the world flaps its wings, which contributes to the causes that make a hurricane on the other side of the planet. Interdependence has a quality of resonance—wave after wave of cause and effect and interaction, often far beyond our comprehension. But it can be felt—and sometimes even photographed. And then felt by looking at the photograph. In other words, it is not far beyond our experience. We experience interdependence, and we know it well. We just don't know what we know.

The visual quality of resonance points to this true quality of reality: the authentic presence of all things interacting. This living sense of authentic presence is a big part of the deep beauty of the images.

Now we have a much deeper and subtler understanding of dot in space. The dot is not simply some *thing* against a background. It is the center of a field of power, manifesting as authentic presence.

This lively and dynamic force field gathers a singularity of reality—the just that/just so. It attracts and holds the eye and mind as it simultaneously radiates and transmits a sensibility. It is a unique transmission of the whole possibility of the phenomenal world. To paraphrase what Chögyam Trungpa says: one can sense the whole vastness and essence of all water in a single dewdrop.

This is not just philosophy: this is the power of just *that* saltshaker, just *that* flower blossom, just *that* psychedelic duck, and all the endless phenomenal dots in space. It is the power of authentic presence, which is the power of now—the power of awake. This is the contemplative way of being awake: contacting realization and joy through the unique power of the phenomenal world.

This is the deeper inner equivalence of any Nalanda Miksang image: the transmission power of now and the transmission power of awake that is grounded in the authentic presence of the moment. This is what your images communicate.

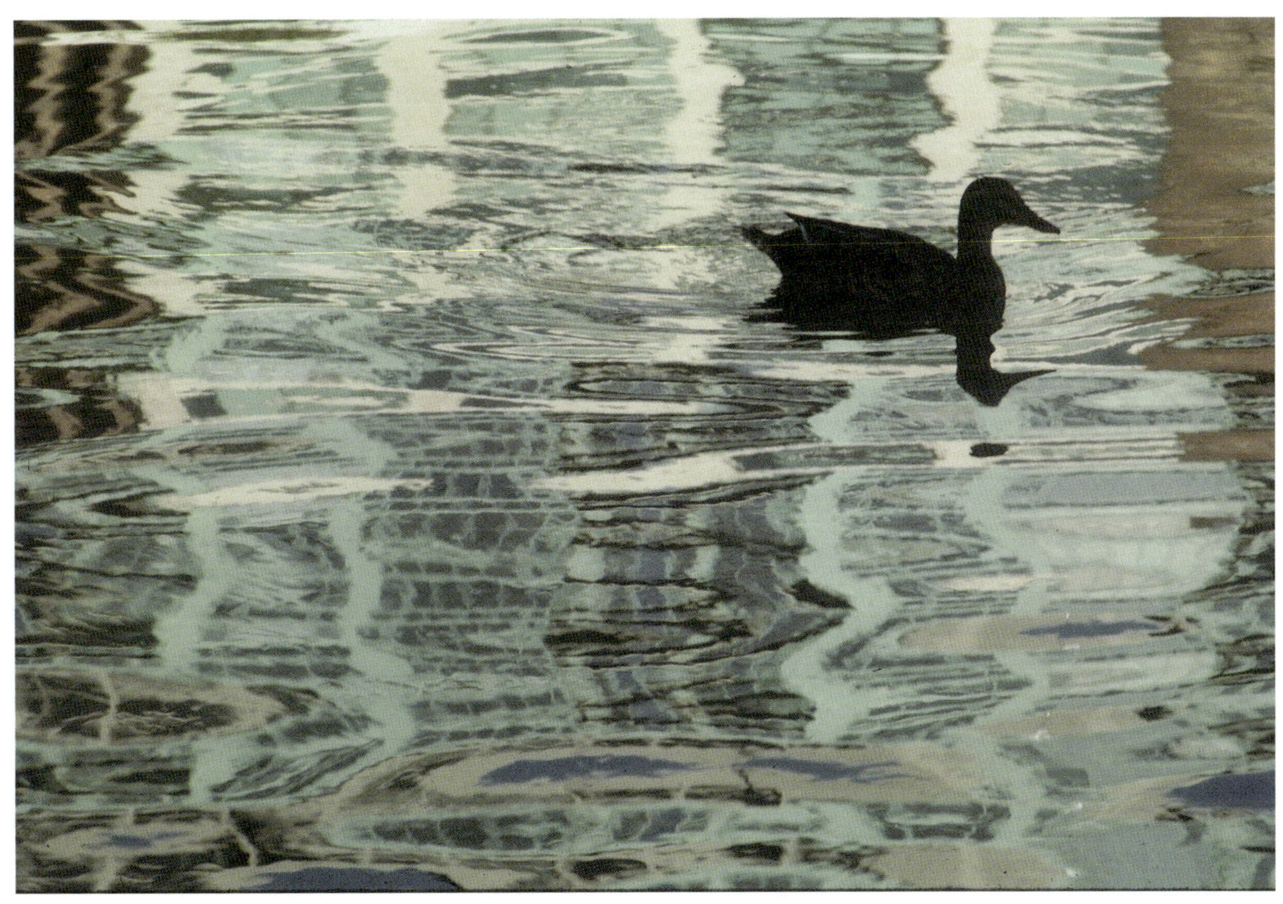

CONCLUSION

The contemplative dimension of Nalanda Miksang is not easy to sum up. This is in part because the contemplative dimension is so intimate; it happens when you become you, as we trust you have already experienced.

And only you can become you. We cannot do that for you.

We hope you have begun to experience the world without the baggage of your interpretative filters of preference and opinion. Don't worry – we all have them. We even need them sometimes. But slowly you can begin to believe that this matrix of preferences and opinions is not "you"—or at least, it's not all of you.

The main practice and the main point is discerning the difference between the "thing world"—taken to be independently and solidly *there*—and the phenomenal world—the uniquely manifested *here*, which is radiant, surprising, and flowing with ordinary magic. Your contact. Your connection. Now.

This is the heart practice. It is the practice of the senses and the sensibilities. It is also the ordinary magic practice; it is how the perception of the everyday ordinary becomes the everyday extraordinary.

As you bridge into level two, you will enter this main teaching.

But there is more—much more. And hopefully, you will experience it as you continue on the path through the Three Levels of Perception, in the next volumes: Volume Two, Fields of Perception and Volume Three, Orderly Chaos - and more. [6]

At the beginning, contemplative photography offers a kind of leverage or skillful means for you to connect with the freshness of the phenomenal world. And on that basis, it helps you make simple yet brilliant photographic images.

Then, at some point, you start to stabilize the "few degrees" solution. You become more oriented to phenomenal display day in and day out. And more and more, the phenomenal world wakes you up.

The special Way of Nalanda Miksang wakes you to the visual radiance of the phenomenal world. What begins as formal practice becomes a natural, everyday event of wakefulness, delight, and creativity.

Now you have entered a potent and exhilarating path of seeing and liberation. Now your contemplative life is your life.

This is the Way of Seeing.

---

6 See further explanations of upcoming assignments in our appendix.

APPENDIX

LEVELS AND TOPICS

LEVEL ONE—FORMS OF PERCEPTION

Level one explores the phenomenal world in a formal way. We break the *thing* world into five basic forms of perception: color, (surface) texture/pattern, light, space, and dot in space.

Level one is inherently abstract. Since we break with the conceptual world, it only consists of flashes of color, light, etc. The fact that we normally relate to things as things serves a great daily purpose for us. But level one lets us investigate another way of relating. The role of level one is to synchronize the eye and camera. It is as close to purely visual as we can get. Level one tends to be up close, precise, and specific. It's very elementary; the color assignment, especially, can feel like primary school.

LEVEL TWO—FIELDS OF PERCEPTION

In level two, we begin to address the deeper view teachings in Nalanda Miksang. We redo dot in space, now exploring how dot in space relates to both how we perceive reality and to actual reality. We photograph dot in space more fully out in the world, letting things be themselves again. There is a sense of things as things, but we cultivate a more perceptual relationship to things.

Level two is less abstract than level one. We recognize the objects in photos almost immediately. But there is also a sense of relationship between the things in the picture, and a connection to us as viewer and photographer. Another way of talking about this is to say that level two has a heart quality—one akin to Zen aesthetics—whose qualities are purity, simplicity, and spaciousness. In level two, we take our synchronized, settled eyes from level one and let them drop through the world, seeing what they see. We are synchronizing not just the eye and camera here, but also the heart. It is important to synchronize the heart as we add in more content and context from the world, so that we keep our purity of seeing from level one and not resort to documentary or thing-based photography. As was the case in level one, level two photographs are photographs of perceptions. This is always our subject: the flash of perception.

In level two, the forms of level one start to appear together. Often a level two shot has strong color, light, texture, space, etc. The flash of perception also often feels physically softer, a bit more diffuse in level two. That is ok. We can still trust it.

We explore level two through topics, which sometimes present themselves in a level one way (a macro flower shot that presents as texture), and sometimes as level two (some part or whole of the flower more fully recognizable and with a heart feeling). During a weekend Nalanda Miksang level two program we cover:

1. Dot in Space (with a level two understanding)

2. Flowers and Weeds

3. Ordinary Personal World

4. Impressionism (natural)

5. People and Other Sentient Beings

Level two also currently contains a second weekend program called Way of Nature, which combines some of the more nature-based topics, like Visual Haiku and Landscape, as well as written haiku. The heart of Nalanda Miksang is in level two.

LEVEL THREE—ORDERLY CHAOS

Level three naturally developed out of the process of practicing levels one and two. We noticed that we'd been following some rules. Though we intended to be open, somehow we'd stumbled upon an aesthetic in levels one and two. Though it is essential to see how we perceive in those levels, and to become stable and have faith in our flash of perception and basic goodness, eventually, most of us start to let in chaos as well. And it has a strong flavor to it.

In level three photographs, we experience visual chaos. Level three pictures tend to make us laugh or shudder or want to look away; they hurt the eyes, cracking our level two sensibilities. And yet, they arise out of flashes of perception.

The introductory (forms) assignments in level three are:

1. Vectors (purposefully letting the eye move around)

2. Paste up (collage)

3. Juxtaposition (collage with juxtaposed content)

Like level two, the fields of level three are endless and include:

4. Stranger in a Strange Land

5. Crime Scene

6. Bardo

ABSOLUTE EYE

We're not sure we know what *Absolute Eye* is. Yet. Like the other areas of Nalanda Miksang, it naturally arose out of shooting. Eventually, after studying chaos, people started to shoot and share photos that were actually quite beautiful pieces of modern art.

Absolute Eye is sort of Nalanda Miksang's sexy, arty cousin.

In Absolute Eye, the mind totally lets go and reaches out into the world. In the first three levels, we bracket our mind, removing it from the process. Here, the mind fully engages and seeks. So photographing Absolute Eye feels different than Nalanda Miksang. The energy changes to that of a two-way relationship instead of the receptive relationship we have with perceptions in the rest of Nalanda Miksang.

We study the New York school of modern art with Absolute Eye. Not just to learn from it but to also try and understand a different view of what they were doing—making perceptual art true to direct experience. The main artists/forms we explore include:

1. Robert Rauschenberg/collage

2. Jackson Pollock/abstract expressionism

3. Mark Rothko/color field

DHARMA TEXTS

Chögyam Trungpa Rinpoche. *True Perception: The Path of Dharma Art.* Shambhala, 2008.
Chögyam Trungpa Rinpoche. *Shambhala: The Sacred Path of the Warrior.* Shambhala, 2007.
Sakyong Mipham. *The Shambhala Principle: Discovery Humanity's Hidden Treasure.* Harmony, 2014.
Sakyong Mipham. *Ruling Your World: Ancient Strategies for Modern Life.* Harmony, 2006.

OTHER RECOMMENDED READINGS:

Karr, Andy and Michael Wood. *The Practice of Contemplative Photography: Seeing the World with Fresh Eyes.* Shambhala, 2011.
DuBose, Julie. *Effortless Beauty: Photography As an Expression of Eye, Mind, and Heart.* Miksang Publications, 2013.
Hayward, Jeremy W. *Letters to Vanessa: On Love, Science, and Awareness in an Enchanted World.* Shambhala, 1997.
Patterson, Freeman. *Photography and the Art of Seeing: A Visual Perception Workshop for Film and Digital Photography.* Firefly Books, 2011.
Loori, John Daido. *Zen of Creativity: Cultivating Your Artistic Life.* Ballantine Books, 2005.
Saitzyk, Steve. *Place Your Thoughts Here: Meditation for the Creative Mind.* First Thought Press, 2013.

ONLINE

It is our intention that this text be accompanied by images on the website for this book, as well as active forums on Flickr and Facebook. Please find us online and participate:

www.miksang.org
www.miksangwayofseeing.com

SOCIAL MEDIA:

Instagram and Twitter: @nalandamiksang
                           @wayofseeing
Facebook: Nalanda Miksang
           Way of Seeing
           (also, location-based groups such as Miksang Texas)
Flickr: Miksang, Way of Seeing, and Miksang Teacher and Student Forum

GLOSSARY

basic goodness: Akin to *bodhicitta*, or a basic open heartedness, basic goodness is a Shambhala teaching that points to the inherent goodness in all humans.

Chögyam Trungpa: Tibetan lama who escaped Tibet in 1959 and eventually came to North America. He founded Shambhala and died in 1986.

cocoon: Our self-constructed mental hiding places where we try to escape the bright shock of reality, good or bad.

contemplation/contemplative: The "outer" meaning is using external media—words, cameras, flowers—as an object in order to directly experience our minds and the world (that appears to be) around us. The "inner" meaning is being one with the sacred and the "secret"meaning is to live in the timeless time. The "temp" of contemplative is the space is the sacred (where they built temples) and also the same source for the "temp" root of time. So deeply, to contemplate is to experience our minds as the sacred timeless time

flash of perception: The naturally occurring, quickly changing action of perception, which changes every millisecond and gives us a fresh experience in every moment.

Meditation: Working directly with breath or other objects to engage the mind and become familiar with its workings.

Nalanda: Ancient Buddhist monastery and school in India. Also used as an umbrella term to describe the contemplative arts in Shambhala Buddhist contexts.

Pema Chodron: An Acharya (senior teacher) in the Shambhala lineage, and a well-known author of many Buddhist books.

perception: Experience of the world and ourselves via our senses.

phenomenal world: The world as we directly experience it through perceptions.

phenomenology: The philosophy of perception and study of "things as they are."

resonance: A Daoist expression of the interdependence of all beings in our world. Akin to the waves of sound or water, each action has an effect on all else in positive or negative ways.

Sakyong: Honorific title given to the core lineage holders in Shambhala, such as Sakyong Mipham and the Druk Sakyong (first Sakyong) Chogyam Trungpa. Means "Earth Protector."

Sakyong Mipham: Current head teacher and lineage holder of Shambhala. Son of Chogyam Trungpa.

Shambhala: A school of Buddhism that comes through Chögyam Trungpa Rinpoche, based in the roots of Kagyu and Nyingma teachings of Tibet and a vision of enlightened society in which all humans recognized their basic goodness. Current leader is Sakyong Mipham Rinpoche.

Vajra Regent: American dharma heir to Chögyam Trungpa in 1976. Died in 1990. Oversaw the development of Miksang photography.

Way: Daoist expression of "things as they are."

A SHORT HISTORY OF MIKSANG AND NALANDA MIKSANG

by John McQuade

All the Miksang teachings emerged the same way. These teachings are not someone's idea. They were not invented or made up. They came through clear seeing. We came to understand and categorize this clear seeing into a step-by-step practice through the insight of Chögyam Trungpa's dharma art teachings.

The development of Miksang had two main supports: the written record of Chögyam Trungpa's dharma art teachings and the guidance of his American dharma heirs or transmission lineage successors.

I have mentioned that the transmission of the Buddha dharma lineages is often mind to mind, warm hand to warm hand, realized teacher to trusted student. Chögyam Trungpa Rinpoche has two dharma heirs: his son, the current Sakyong Mipham Rinpoche, and Thomas Rich, the Vajra Regent Osel Tendzin.

After Chögyam Trungpa presented the dharma art teachings, Vajra Regent Osel Tendzin, an amateur photographer, established a group of photographers in Boulder to explore the teachings through that medium. He called this early photographic group *Miksang.*

Meanwhile, Michael Wood, a professional photographer, began meditation practice. He explored the possibility of merging the experience of meditation perception with the medium of photography. He presented a course based on this exploration. The assignments focused on color, light, and texture. To this day, Wood's assignments remain the level one Miksang assignments.

In the same time period, I was a graduate student studying a contemporary philosophy called *phenomenology.* The *ology* is from the Greek *logos,* a Western way to study things as they are. *Phenomenon* are observable facts or events. So phenomenology is the way of distinguishing things as they are by observation. It is that simple—except it is philosophy, so it is expressed in a complex way. As I studied, I wondered how someone could bring together the experience of meditation with the understanding of phenomenology. I wondered how phenomenology could be something like haiku: a simple, direct, but profound expression.

My at the time girlfriend, Alice Yang, now my wife, was a friend of Michael's. She took the first course he offered. At the conclusion of the course, they presented a show, and when I saw that show, I realized it was perception. It was dharma. It was what I had been looking for. I joined Michael in exploring this way. We contacted the Vajra Regent Osel Tendzin, who oversaw the development of this way of seeing. He officially named what we were doing *Miksang.* In this way, what are now known as the official Miksang teachings emerged.

Just to be crystal clear: Miksang teachings are not something that came from Michael or myself. They are the ways of pure perception. Some of the pedagogy draws on our insights, but it also draws on the ways dharma is taught, and from the pure experience of the practice itself.

In 1985, we felt that the Miksang pedagogy and path was in place and presented this to the Vajra Regent Osel Tendzin. He approved it with two conditions: that we write a ninefold logic, and that we establish a Miksang society with an executive council.

Traditional Dharma presentations often involve threefold logic. Typically these are named *ground, path*, and *fruition*. The Miksang pedagogy that we presented to the Vajra Regent had three stages, based on a dharma art teaching of Chögyam Trungpa called the Three Levels of Perception. He wanted the detailed version: each of the levels needed to be threefold. I wrote the ninefold logic, the Vajra Regent approved it, and to this day, it is the View of Nalanda Miksang.

I now understand the wisdom of this requirement. A real contemplative art practice cannot be based on only personal intuition and creativity. It must be based on some time-tested form in order to express things as they are. Our intention in these Nalanda contemplative photography teachings is to present a way to explore things as they are.

The executive and society requirements were more ambiguous. In retrospect, it's clear that I did not understand the deep insight and vision in these requirements. I regarded them as practicalities. We set up a Miksang executive council: president, John McQuade; education, Michael Wood; and secretary, Margaret Thurlow.

Nalanda Miksang has evolved since then, through the teachings of Sakyong Mipham Rinpoche and the projects of Nalanda Miksang teacher Miriam Hall, to begin to manifest a specific understanding of contemplative art. It has an impact beyond individual experience, craft, and image, and it empowers the life situations of many people and, as a contemplative art, enriches human culture.

So Nalanda Miksang is not just a set of teachings about making contemplative images. First, it was a contemplative school whose distinctive view, pedagogy, and organization formed naturally. There was no grand plan: it just found its way in the world, with some help from humans. For example, at some point it became clear that the worldwide interest in Miksang could only be served through establishing more teachers, so I offered a teacher training program. The number of Nalanda Miksang teachers began to increase, throughout North America and the rest of the world. These teachers, in turn, infused and continue to infuse the culture of Nalanda Miksang with their own unique expressions. In order to gather and share this collective wisdom, we have recently instituted a yearly retreat for Nalanda Miksang teachers. The Nalanda Miksang society develops in this manner.

CAMERA CRAFT SUGGESTIONS

As we state many times during the book, Nalanda Miksang focuses more on perception than photography—and yet, we are making photographs! The craft of photography—focus, exposure, etc.—affects how clearly our perceptions come across. So we also wish to make sure you have some of your basics down.

CAMERA TYPES

Three basic levels of digital cameras are available. They are listed below, from beginner to professional. If you aren't sure what you want for your work, you can use this to figure out which kind of camera you are using or what range of camera you would like to buy.

1. **Point-and-shoot (compact) cameras** are likely what you have if you have never even heard of another kind of camera. They are compact cameras with built-in lenses and many automatic (possibly all automatic) settings. They are good starting cameras.

2. **Mirrorless or DSLM (Digital Single Lens Mirrorless) cameras** are a newer form of digital camera. They are still fairly lightweight and more comparable in body size to point-and-shoot cameras, while having interchangeable lenses and more manual control (like the DSLR, see below).

3. **DSLR (Digital Single Lens Reflex) cameras** are for folks who like to have options for full manual control. Once you enter into this realm of larger-bodied, fuller-framed cameras, the sky is the limit. While entry-level, nonprofessional versions of DSLRs are available, the cost points for basic kits make them inaccessible to most people, not to mention the complexity of their operation.

A NOTE ON CAMERA TYPES

We have not listed camera phones because, as of publication, we find that folks taking our courses have to make too many post-processing adjustments if they use camera phones. Or they say things like, "My flash of perception was that flower, but I couldn't get close enough with my phone." So current phone cameras still have serious limitations. As well, settings in camera phones vary too far to cover here.

Does this mean you can't use your phone to shoot Nalanda Miksang? No. But we highly suggest trying cameras that give you a little more freedom. To find pointers for when phone cameras have more control, or to work with the limitations of your phone, you can check on our website or later editions of the book. For camera phones, follow our suggestions as much as they are helpful.

Also, a basic digital course is tremendously useful and much more appealing than reading the manual if you are new to your camera. Try a course online or at your local community college. That being said, you may need your manual for some of these adjustments. What is nice about digital photography is that we can learn faster and see our results right away.

SUGGESTIONS FOR EVERYONE

1. **Wear a hat or shield your screen with your hand so you can see what you are shooting.** Small point-and-shoot cameras (and even some DSLRs) have LCD screens that can be impossible to see in the sun. More and more cameras don't have viewfinders at all. Camera stores sell little devices you can use to shield your screen when the sun is bright. Try one of those if you are having a hard time.

2. **Do not use a flash.** Every camera can turn off its flash. The purpose of flash is to wash out light variations, which winds up washing out color as well. It also causes odd reflections and shadows as a side effect.

3. **Start where you are.** If you are new to your camera, work with automatic or semiautomatic settings. If you have used your camera a long time, take on a more challenging aspect of an assignment or try to use manual settings.

4. **Generally, if you can, shoot early morning or late afternoon.** This is when natural light is the most interesting and nuanced. Photographers call these times the magic hours—especially early evening. It's not that you can't shoot or it won't turn out with the midday sun, but midday sun is flatter, as we see in the light assignment. It washes out more details of texture and lighting, and even dulls color.

5. **Don't shoot indoors.** Indoor light is much harder to work with, especially if you are new to shooting. The light is uneven, sometimes of mixed or low quality, and harder to expose for. The exception might be sunlight coming inside. Still, working outside is best, and, dare we say, most fitting for our training.

6. **Low light equals blurry pictures, unless you have a tripod or a very steady hand.** If you have a manual camera, you can adjust your settings. Point-and-shoots also include some settings you can adjust (see below for both). You can also use a tripod. If you are tripod-less, lean against something when shooting—use a tree trunk or stump or even the ground as a tripod replacement. If you have an automatic camera, you may have to give up a shot if it will be too blurry.

7. **Overall note on light, especially for Point-and-Shoots:** Our aperture and further light assignment suggestions are really only useful for people using cameras with some manual control over light setting. If you are using a point-and-shoot, you do have an EV +/- setting you can use to overall expose the scene brighter or darker, which may help some with the light assignments but is too general to be as precise as manual control.

8. **Which all leads to the most important point of all: If you are struggling to get a shot, let it go.** Give your flash of perception one or two tries. If you haven't gotten the perception after that, move on. It can be hard to do, but it is an important part of the practice. Do not plan on Photoshopping—let yourself be totally present to the shoot, working with what is. As we like to say in Nalanda Miksang workshops: if you are going to post-process an image, it's much easier to crop or adjust a clear equivalent of a perception than an unclear one.

BASIC CAMERA SETTINGS

1. **Set the ISO to 200 or 400**—400 will make it easier to shoot in less light but still be in focus. Most point-and-shoots default to 100 for the ISO. This makes nearly every photo blurry, unless you are in bright light.

2. **If you are shooting indoors, change your white balance**—auto white balance does a pretty good job outdoors. However, if you shoot with indoor light, you can't trust the auto white balance. Have you ever taken pictures inside only to have them turn out much redder or bluer than you thought? Set your white balance to match the main light source in the room. On point-and-shoots, white balance icons show, at minimum, a choice between incandescent bulbs versus florescent bulbs. If you are using a DSLR or DSLM, you may also be able to set according to temperature (Kelvin). Don't bother with this unless you cannot seem to get it right with the icon settings.

3. **If you are shooting a close-up, set your camera to macro mode (the tiny flower mode) or to portrait mode (the profile of a face icon/ head-and-shoulders icon).** These modes are there to help your camera focus more on details. In fact, close-up flower shots are often called Macros. Macro is good for texture and closer-in shots of parts of things, parts of flowers, grass, etc. Portrait mode focuses on whatever is in the center of your picture, leaving the background less in focus. Portrait mode in particular is good for perceptions that have the middle distance front in focus and the background out of focus.

4. **If you are shooting a far-off field or something at a distance, turn to landscape mode (usually a mountain-shaped icon).**

5. **Feel free to use optical zoom, but avoid digital zoom.** Digital zoom makes shots pixilated or choppy, and you lose quality quickly. Only use optical zoom. You can turn off digital zoom in your menu.

6. **Point-and-shoot cameras do well with color and pattern, space and dot-in-space assignments.** We all have limits, in our lives, as well as our cameras! Some of your peers with bigger cameras and more manual control will deliver better equivalents of texture or light. The key is to get to know what your camera can and can't do, and work within those limits. Become familiar with yours and play within them.

7. **If you have a point-and-shoot that has aperture priority setting, or any options other than preselected Landscape, Portrait, etc., please see below for more setting suggestions.**

BASIC CAMERA SETTINGS –ADVANCED

1. **If you are brand-new to your camera, just work with automatic.** Don't be ashamed. It's OK! The great part about digital cameras and DSLM and DSLR in particular is that the data about the images is saved with your image, so you can learn by looking back later at what your camera chose.

2. **Auto or manual focus.** This depends on your comfort level. If you want control over your focus, you'll need to do manual. Check out options for how to meter your focus on your camera. Some common options are center weighted (whatever is in the center is in focus), overall focus (best for long distance/landscape), or select focus (you choose where in the frame the focus is). Whether you are using manual or auto focus, the camera will usually tell you when

what you want is in focus. A green box, a light in your viewfinder/screen, or lights just above your screen are the common indicators. A red light or box means it is out of focus.

3. **If you want a bit more manual control but are not used to your new camera, we recommend aperture priority.** This setting allows you to manually choose aperture and automatically adjusts your shutter speed for you. Aperture priority also allows for the adjustments stated in basic camera settings: white balance and ISO.

4. **More on aperture—It always seems tricky, but here's a simple breakdown. This is best done via aperture priority to start.**

   a. **If you are shooting something far away, or a situation in which you want everything in focus, you can set the aperture at any number above F16.** If you want to have something in focus and the fore- or background (both, and/or) out of focus, you'll need F11 or under. In other words, the larger the aperture number, the more items in your photo will be in focus. The smaller the number, the fewer parts will be in focus. For instance, if you want to shoot an up-close flower and get as much of it in focus as you can, therefore, set your aperture to F16 or above. Make sure your camera confirms that it can focus that close and also at that aperture. The trick with aperture is that you need lots of light for the larger numbers and less light for lower numbers. If you only want one part of the flower in focus (say, a bud in focus and the whole background out of focus), you'll need to be well under F11. Experiment and you'll see what we mean.

   b. **If you are not using aperture priority, then you'll also need to set your shutter speed.** Generally, you want shutter speed to balance out your aperture. The bigger the aperture number, the smaller the shutter speed.

5. **On metering for available light.**

You can actually use your hand as a good gray card. A gray card was a traditional tool to figure out exposure for your manual camera. Different colors require distinct amounts of light to be exposed properly. So if you are shooting concrete, for instance, the light gets sucked in and the camera overexposes to compensate.

The opposite is true with a bright situation—if it's very sunny and the area around your shot is white, the camera will underexpose.

To solve either situation, put your hand in the light your subject is in, palm up, and spot expose for your hand. You'll see the light meter will jump a lot from what you are seeing, unless you are shooting grass (which is quite close to middle gray). That is the reading to set your shutter speed to.

This is not an exact science. If you want to get really technical (and some of you will), the palm of your hand is one stop brighter than a gray card (this crosses all skin colors). In order to get the light just right, you need to add a stop. For instance, if you want it at F11, you'll need to change it to F16.

EXPOSING LIGHT AND SURFACE ASSIGNMENTS

Patches of Light/Shadow

Let's say you have a flash of perception of a patch of light.

Take your reading from the patch of light—what you perceived, not the whole scene. If you expose for the whole scene, the camera will average the exposure between the light and shadow. Recall that we are working with perception and you are trying to form an equivalent of that perception.

By exposing for just the light, the camera captures the contrast between light and shadow. This highlights the edge of the contrast. Then, your image is a strong equivalent of a patch of light, presenting light as light.

Make your f-stop decisions so the image will be a definite and pure equivalent. Then move to the light on the wall, and take your meter reading. Finally, move back to the framing place. Ignore your meter reading and make the image. The image will be a patch of light on a larger surface.

This is the basic approach. Some situations require a refinement. For instance, you may not be able to fill the frame with the flash of perception: the patch of light may be too small, up close, or too far away. Here you need to understand the principle of the approach and not just the mechanics. The key is making an exposure that replicates the light on the surface one is photographing. For example, if it is large patch of light on a wall across a yard enclosed by a fence, then you take a light reading from where you are when you have the flash. The light falls in the same direction on you and the wall, so take your reading of something else that is available and on the same plane as the wall. Then the exposure will be the same. The fence is not the issue. You don't need to go up to the surface you are photographing. Just make an exposure that replicates the conditions of light. It's the same with small patches of light. Cameras want to average out the light and dark, erasing the patches you want to expose for. Instead, find a place where you can replicate the angle and reflection. Then go back to the place where you frame the perception and take your photo.

There is no formula for this. It depends on the perception and how you want to craft the image. Generally, you are still exposing for the light. Generally, the light is the major focus of the perception and the shadow area is a support or context. A good approach is to expose for the light. Use that as a baseline and then open from there, letting in more light a little at a time, maybe a half stop.

Backlighting

In general, position yourself with your back to the sun, or light source, so that you are backlit. In this position, find a neutral green object or surface (grass) or one colored similarly to what you are shooting. Set your light settings for this light; then turn around and focus and take your shot. The camera will not like this idea. It only works with a fully manual camera. The trick with light and cameras is that cameras want to average out light and dark, which is why your flash goes off automatically in dark situations. In this moment, however, you are attempting to capture the contrast, not the similarity. Again, work with bracketing the image if this helps you at first.

Texture

In terms of craft, use as much depth of field as possible to represent texture. This increases the contrast between light and shadow and highlights and depths. Set your shutter speed at the lowest you can hand hold (usually 30) and adjust the depth of field as deep as the exposure will allow.

On Bracketing

The light aspect of craft comes with experience, through trial and error. If you are a beginner in terms of camera craft, you might want to bracket in some of these situations. Bracketing is making more than one exposure of a subject in a systematic way: half stop open; half stop closed. Generally, in contemplative photography, we don't encourage this. Bracketing can undermine your confidence in the long run. You don't learn the craft; you actually begin to embody the doubt that you don't know how to do it. So you compensate for your doubt by bracketing.

Still, special circumstances require special means. At the beginning, it might be helpful to bracket. If you do this, make sure you look at the information from the exposures on your digital files so that you can learn from the comparisons. Bracketing is training wheels. Once you find your balance, you can let them go.

Much of the training in contemplative photography is actually mind training. You train to be genuine and free. Training in the craft and training the mind go together.

CREDITS

Excerpts from *Shambhala: The Sacred Path of the Warrior*, by Chögyam Trungpa; © 1984 by Chögyam Trungpa. Reprinted by arrangement with Shambhala Publications, Inc., Boston, MA. www.shambhala.com.

Excerpt from *The Shambhala Principle: Discovering Humanity's Hidden Treasure* by Sakyong Mipham, copyright © 2013 by Mipham J. Mukpo. Used by permission of Harmony Books, an imprint of the Crown Publishing Group, a division of Random House LLC. All rights reserved.

Excerpt from *Ruling Your World: Ancient Strategies For Modern Life* by Sakyong Mipham, copyright © 2005 by Sakyong Mipham. Used by permission of Broadway Books, an imprint of the Crown Publishing Group, a division of Random House LLC. All rights reserved.

ABOUT THE AUTHORS

John McQuade is one of the founders of Miksang Contemplative Photography, which he has presented for thirty years. He is the most senior teacher of the Nalanda Miksang school. John is a long time meditator, meditation instructor, and Shambhala Training director in the Shambhala tradition. He practices Daoist Qi-gong and writes on the contemplative arts. He holds an M.A in Phenomenology and a PhD in Social and Political Thought.

Miriam Hall is a contemplative arts teacher who lives in Madison, Wisconsin, and travels internationally to teach Nalanda Miksang, Shambhala Art, and contemplative writing. She is the second most senior teacher under John McQuade in the Nalanda Miksang School. She has been teaching these practices for over ten years and deeply enjoys committing her livelihood to them. For more information on her courses and philosophy, visit www.herspiral.com.